D1502029

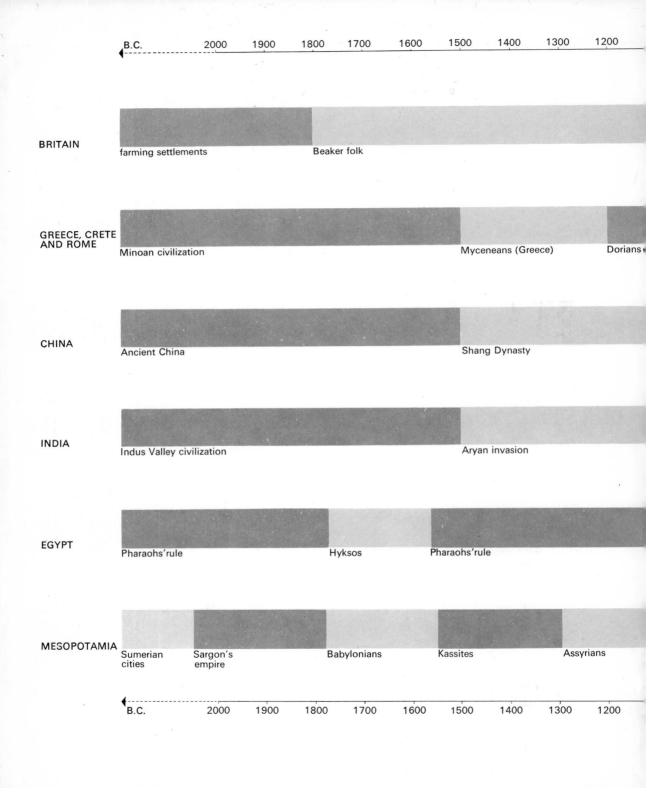

B.C.   2000   1900   1800   1700   1600   1500   1400   1300   1200

BRITAIN
farming settlements   Beaker folk

GREECE, CRETE AND ROME
Minoan civilization   Myceneans (Greece)   Dorians

CHINA
Ancient China   Shang Dynasty

INDIA
Indus Valley civilization   Aryan invasion

EGYPT
Pharaohs' rule   Hyksos   Pharaohs' rule

MESOPOTAMIA
Sumerian   Sargon's   Babylonians   Kassites   Assyrians
cities   empire

B.C.   2000   1900   1800   1700   1600   1500   1400   1300   1200

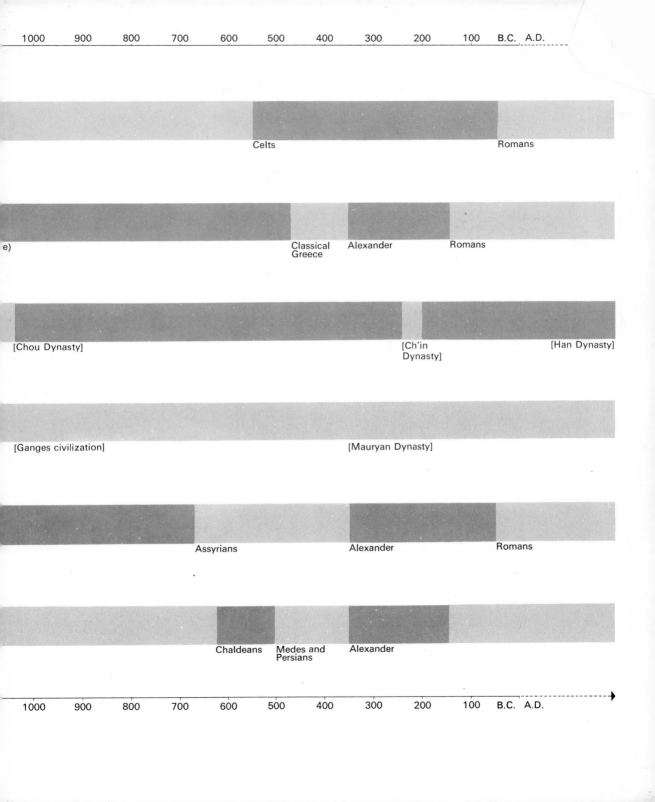

1000 900 800 700 600 500 400 300 200 100 B.C. A.D.

Celts   Romans

e)   Classical   Alexander   Romans
                                Greece

[Chou Dynasty]   [Ch'in   [Han Dynasty]
                                                  Dynasty]

[Ganges civilization]   [Mauryan Dynasty]

Assyrians   Alexander   Romans

Chaldeans   Medes and   Alexander
             Persians

1000 900 800 700 600 500 400 300 200 100 B.C. A.D.

Penguin Education

Out of the Ancient World

Victor Skipp

Victor Skipp, who was educated at Bury Grammar School, Lancashire, and at Emmanuel College, Cambridge, was Head of the History Department of Sheldon Heath Comprehensive School, Birmingham. He joined the staff of the new Bordesley Day College of Education in 1964, where he is Principal Lecturer in History and Head of the Department of Environmental Studies.

A History of Britain

Out of the Ancient World

Victor Skipp

Penguin Education

Design: Arthur Lockwood

Illustration research: Naomi H. Jacoby

Penguin Education, Penguin Books Ltd, Harmondsworth, Middlesex, England
Penguin Books Inc., 7110 Ambassador Road, Baltimore, Md 21207, U.S.A.
Penguin Books Australia Ltd, Ringwood, Victoria, Australia
Penguin Books Canada Ltd, 41 Steelcase Road West, Markham, Ontario, Canada
Penguin Books (N.Z.) Ltd, 182-190 Wairau Road, Auckland 10, New Zealand

First published 1967
Reprinted 1968, 1970, 1971, 1973, 1975, 1976
Copyright © Victor Skipp, 1967

Printed in Hong Kong by Sheck Wah Tong Printing Press
Set in Lumitype Plantin

This book is sold subject to the condition that it shall not, by way of trade or otherwise, be
lent, re-sold, hired out, or otherwise circulated without the publisher's prior consent in any
form of binding or cover other than that in which it is published and without a similar
condition including this condition being imposed on the subsequent purchaser

Contents

Preface

My overriding concern has been to provide an account of the main formative developments: such as the origins of man, the discovery of farming, the invention of metallurgy and writing, the building of the first cities, the evolution of rational thought and scientific method, the growth of democracy. I have also tried to show how some of these ideas and techniques reached our own country, so that the reader may begin to see the extent to which Britain was born *Out of the Ancient World*.

At the same time it has not seemed enough to restrict attention to Western origins: today's oecumenical perspectives require that something be said – however briefly – of the civilizations of India and China.

A word is due about the factual content of the book. Great efforts have been made – by others as well as myself – to see that it is based on the latest evidence. New methods of scientific dating have recently suggested that many pre-historic developments took place much earlier than had been previously supposed, and the revised dates have been adopted. This means that readers using the books recommended at the end of chapters will sometimes meet with discrepancies, since most of them still use the old chronologies; even the dates I have used cannot be considered final.

In other respects also the facts cited – particularly in the earlier chapters – need to be regarded with caution. Every year archaeological discoveries are made and experts adjust their views.

Since this book was first published in 1967 there has been a further dating revolution. From the early 1950s the chief way of determining pre-historic dates was by the radiocarbon (C 14) method. Recent work on radiocarbon dating, however, suggests that these radiocarbon dates are too low. Thus a radiocarbon date of 2000 B.C. ought probably to be revised to 2500 B.C.; and radiocarbon dates of 3200 B.C. to 4000 B.C. Such an adjustment in chronology poses many problems for scholars, and it has therefore been decided not to revise the dates originally used in this book for the time being. Nevertheless readers may like to bear in mind this general trend towards earlier dating.

Chapter 1
Man the hunter

There are many ways in which man is different from the lower animals. But one of the most important ways is that he has greater powers of thought. He has ideas, flashes of inspiration, he is constantly making inventions and discoveries.

Animals do not invent tools in the way that the human race does. It is true that they have 'tools'. The front feet of the mole are marvellous for digging. But they are not 'tools' in our sense. The mole's feet are part of the mole. Man, by contrast, uses tools which are not part of himself, but which he has invented and made.

This idea of making tools gives him a tremendous advantage over animals. The mole can dig well with his feet, but they would not be much good for knocking in a nail! With his hands alone man may not be able to dig as well as the mole. But to make up for this he invented the spade, and later the plough and the bulldozer. Besides, unlike the mole, when he has finished digging, he can put his hands to other purposes. With other tools he can screw in a screw, write a letter, or even fly through the air.

Everybody today can light a fire; but no animal knows how to do it. Think of the hundreds of ways we use fire: for warmth, lighting and cooking; for smelting metals, making bricks, tiles and pottery; for driving steam-engines, internal combustion-engines, and producing various other forms of power.

Where should we be today without the use of tools or fire? It is doubtful whether our way of life would differ very much from that of other animals. Obviously then, the man, or man-like creature, who picked up a piece of stone or wood and out of it shaped the first crude tool was making a momentous discovery. So was the man who first used fire.

Prehistory and archaeology

If we are interested in the beginnings of the human story, with its important early discoveries, 'history' does not reach back far enough for us. Strictly speaking 'history' only begins when our ancestors had learned to write. From then onwards they kept a record of some of their actions and thoughts and so left an account of themselves for the future. But this started to happen

Drawing of
Southern ape-man

The archaeologist, Dr Louis Leakey, excavating in Tanzania for clues of early man. This has to be done with care, using such implements as tiny chisels, camel-hair brushes and tooth-picks.

not much more than 5,000 years ago. The vast stretch of man s development which comes before this we call 'prehistory', meaning 'before history'.

A hundred years ago hardly anything was known about this early period. There is still a great deal that we do not know and will never know. What information we have comes from the skilful and painstaking study of the chance remains left by our remote ancestors: their own bones, the bones of the animals they hunted for meat, their living sites, the primitive tools they used, and so on. Most of these remains are found buried in the earth and the science of discovering and studying them is called 'archaeology'.

Southern ape-man

Although it is certain that we share a common ancestor with the ape, experts are still unable to say exactly how man evolved. They are searching for new evidence all the time, but until more skulls and skeletons are found there will remain many important gaps in the story.

Apes are tropical creatures, so it is not surprising that Africa seems to have been the birthplace of the human race. Here the separation of man's ancestors from those of the ape may have taken place as much as 20,000,000 years ago, which would mean that we are cousins of the ape a million or more times removed.

Between 2,000,000 and 500,000 years ago, the so-called Southern ape, or ape-man, was living in Africa. His brain was no bigger than that of a modern ape, while his head retained many ape-like features, such as a thick overhanging brow-ridge and a heavy projecting jaw. By contrast, ape-man's body was quite human. He stood about four feet in height – the size of a modern pigmy – and walked upright on two legs, so that his arms were free for other purposes.

Traces of Southern ape-man have been found in several parts of Africa, but it is at the Oldoway (Olduvai) Gorge in Tanzania that some of the most important discoveries have come to light. Here, also, were excavated the remains of what Dr Leakey, their discoverer, believes to be a more advanced creature, who was living at Oldoway about 1,700,000 years ago, perhaps with Southern ape-men as his neighbours. Some people think that this creature is sufficiently man-like to be counted as human; and Dr Leakey, because he regards him as the earliest known tool-maker, has named him Handy man.

Handy man's tools were crudely chipped pebbles (see right) which he probably used to skin and cut up the meat of antelope and other small animals he hunted. On his living-site, which was by the side of a lake, the excavators also found a number of large stones, some piled on top of one another, and arranged in a semi-circle. These may have formed a primitive hut or windbreak.

Handy man, however, was only announced in 1964 and experts are still arguing about his proper place in the human story. Some think he is merely another type of Southern ape-man, and even question whether he made the tools. Perhaps, they say, the tools were made by the ape-men who were his neighbours; and this is quite possible, for pebble tools have been found at several other ape-man sites.

Erect man

The Southern ape-men were dying out roughly 500,000 years ago, but by this time another man-like creature had developed, known to archaeologists as Erect man. Although he also may have originated in tropical Africa, Erect man later spread into southern Asia and parts of Europe. For instance, he is known to have lived in central China and Hungary, places where he had to adapt himself to a temperate climate.

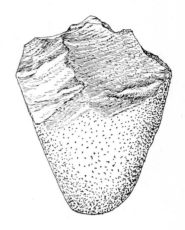

Early pebble tool from Oldoway. A sharp ridge has been formed at one end of the pebble by knocking off a few flakes from each side.

Early hand-axe. Like the pebble tool, this comes from Oldoway, but was excavated at a higher level and dates from over a million years later, i.e. roughly the same period as the Peking chopper.

Peking men at the mouth of their cave.

Peking chopper. This type of tool is thought to have been made as shown in the illustration above. A suitable stone or piece of rock was placed on an 'anvil' and flakes chipped away by striking it with a hammer-stone.

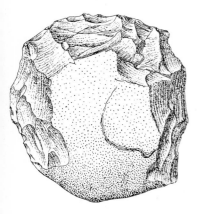

From the skulls and skeletons of about forty individuals excavated in caves near Peking we know that when fully grown these people stood about five feet tall. They had low receding foreheads, a pronounced ridge over the eyes, broad, flat noses and large, almost chinless jaws. But if their facial appearance remained rather ape-like, their brains were twice the size of the Southern ape-man's. Moreover, serving this enlarged brain, Erect men had hands that were more pliant and adaptable than those of any earlier creature.

They made tools of stone, particularly of flint and quartzite, which could be chipped easily. As you can see from the illustration (near left), the choppers made about 350,000 years ago by the Peking men were still rather crude; but at Oldoway and other places in Africa better stone tools were already being made: a large flint was chipped away until it was oval or pear-shaped, with sharp, if rather jagged, cutting edges on each side. Such tools are called hand-axes (far left).

Men of this time doubtless used clubs and spears made of wood, but since wood rots so easily there is little chance of these surviving. However, the end of a yew spear which dates from between 400,000 and 300,000 years ago has been found at

Clacton-on-Sea, Essex (see illustration). The people who made it are believed to have been among the earliest human inhabitants of Britain. But since none of their bones have yet been discovered, it is impossible to say whether they were Erect men or not.

One important step forward taken by some Erect men was the use of fire. As far as we know, the ape-men of Africa did not use it. But Peking men, living in a colder climate, kept fires for warming their caves and probably for simple cooking; archaeologists came across their hearths.

Since all animals are frightened of fire, it may also have been used in hunting. Parties of men may have come upon an animal and, shouting and waving their flaring torches, driven it towards a simple trap they had prepared; or towards a bog, where its limbs would sink into the mud; or perhaps over a precipice.

End of a yew spear from Clacton-on-Sea. *Right:* a flint 'spoke-shave' found nearby which may have been used for shaping spears and other wooden implements.

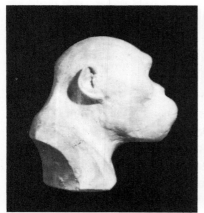

Southern ape-man

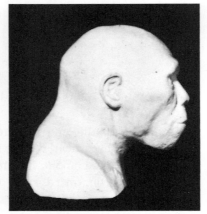

Erect man: Peking

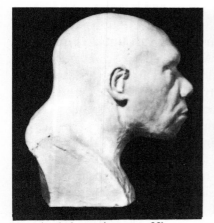

Neanderthal man (see page 22)

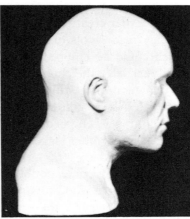

Modern man

Stages in the evolution of man. Reconstructed heads showing the changing profile. Notice the differences in the jaw and in the brow ridges.

Whatever their methods, Erect men were probably able to outwit even the largest animals. Among the meat bones found in the Peking caves are those not only of deer, antelope, wild pig and bison, but also of elephant and rhinoceros.

Apart from tool-making and the use of fire, speech was another important early development. Through speech men can convey their thoughts to each other, talk over past events, and discuss plans for the future. This enables them to work together. With speech, the older members of a group can explain to the younger all that experience has taught them, thereby ensuring that the slowly growing body of human discoveries would be handed on down the generations. Whether Peking man had learned to speak or not, no one knows for certain. But some archaeologists think he would have had a simple kind of language, even if it consisted merely of grunts and gestures.

The Ice Ages

From before the time of Erect man to about 10,000 years ago the earth was at intervals in the grip of the Ice Ages. For tens of thousands of years ice sheets and glaciers, thousands of feet thick, covered most of the northern parts of America, Asia and Europe. In England the ice sometimes came as far down as the Thames. Even farther south, walls of blue ice spread out from such mountain ranges as the Pyrenees, the Alps and the Himalayas. With each invasion of ice, the world of early man shrank towards the equator until almost a third of the earth's land surface was ice-covered. Woolly rhinoceroses, wolves and mammoths wandered over Britain.

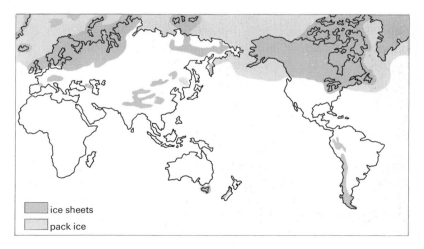

Area of the world's surface covered by ice during the Ice Ages.

ice sheets
pack ice

Thousands of years later, conditions gradually began to improve. Slowly – at the rate of about a quarter of a mile each year – the huge ice masses melted and withdrew. The northern parts of the world became habitable again. Indeed, during the interglacial periods the climate was sometimes sufficiently warm for elephants and hippopotami to live as far north as Norfolk.

The ice sheets advanced and retreated four times in all, which means that there were four Ice Ages and three interglacial periods (see page 23).

Man the hunter

Throughout the Ice Ages, man's only way of keeping himself alive was by hunting wild animals and collecting plant foods, such as edible roots, nuts, fruits and berries. No one had yet discovered how to sow and cultivate corn, or any other crop. No one had tamed any animals. Farming had simply not been thought of. This long period is therefore the period of man the hunter.

Because most of the tools and weapons – or, at any rate, most of those which have survived – were made of stone, we call it the Old Stone Age.

First true men?

Through his stone implements we can trace some small part of early man's progress in skill. But progress was extremely slow. It was as slow as the movement of the ice! Thousands of years might pass without there being a single discovery or improvement. A hundred generations would come and go, and man's way of life would remain exactly the same. Contrast this with the feverish speed at which things change and develop today!

As we have seen, the first hand-axes were made in Africa, but later their use spread to Europe and Asia. Gradually, too, men became increasingly skilful at making them (see right). The later hand-axes are elegant almond-shaped objects, with a sharp point at one end and two knife-like cutting edges (see front cover). No one had yet had the idea of fixing such implements into wooden handles, so to work with them the butt, or thick end, had to be grasped in the hand.

Nevertheless the later hand-axes were fine tools, capable of being used for many different purposes: for grubbing up roots, killing animals, carving meat, scraping skins, cutting and shaping wood, even for felling trees (see page 22). They were so useful that for a very long time hardly any other types of stone tool were made. The hand-axe was the answer to everything.

Development of methods in making stone implements.
1 By banging one stone against another. The Oldoway pebble tool was made in this way and Peking men used a similar method, except that they rested the tool to be worked upon an 'anvil' stone.
2 and 3 Later in the Old Stone Age flakes were removed more accurately by pressing hard on the stone in the right place. You could try these methods with suitable flints.

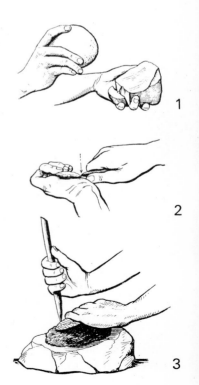

The men who perfected the hand-axe are the earl[y]
whose skulls and brain size are closely similar to our ow[n].
experts think that they should be regarded as the first true men
(*Homo sapiens*), though others insist that there is not enough
evidence to be sure.

Parts of the skull of one of these people were dug up in a
gravel pit at Swanscombe in Kent, with some hand-axes and the
remains of red deer, rhinoceros and elephant close by. Swanscombe man is the oldest human inhabitant of Britain whose bones
have been found. He is thought to have been living during one
of the warm interglacial periods, perhaps about 250,000 years
ago: i.e. roughly 100,000 years after the Clacton men.

Although no other skulls or skeletons of the hand-axe makers
have so far been discovered in this country, a good number of
their hand-axes have been found. You would be able to see one
at any large museum.

Modern men

It was about 35,000 years ago that men of modern type first
appeared. This was in the middle of the final Ice Age when the
ice had spread out over much of the northern hemisphere for

Swanscombe men on a hunting
expedition. Like the drawing of
Peking men, this is a
reconstruction.

Three inventions of the late Old Stone Age.

1   Barbed harpoon for catching fish. (What was the idea of the barbs?)

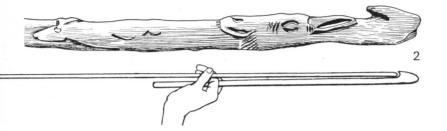

2   Spear-thrower, with a drawing showing how it was used. The spear-thrower was probably invented before the bow and gave the spear greater force and range.

3

3   Cave painting in Spain showing men hunting stags with bows and arrows. This is a drawing, as the original is too difficult to photograph.

Below: a ceremonial staff made of antler from the Cheddar Gorge.

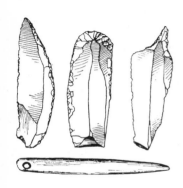

Flint tools of the late Old Stone Age. *Left:* a knife; *centre:* a scraper; *right:* a piercer or **boring tool**; *below:* a bone needle.

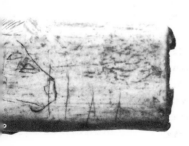

Horse's head on a rib bone from Creswell Crags. This is one of the few pieces of Old Stone Age art found in Britain. If there were ever any cave paintings our damp climate has caused them to flake away.

the last time. On page 23 is a picture of the skull of one men, and if you compare it with that of Erect man, notice the difference. In fact it is virtually indistinguishable one of our own skulls. So, although there is still doubt about whether men of the Swanscombe type were completely human, these modern men certainly were.

In many ways modern men went on living the same life as before. Most of them still made their homes in caves; all depended on game-hunting for their livelihood. But we can tell from their tools and weapons that they had more advanced ideas than their predecessors, as well as being far cleverer with their hands. For instance, instead of relying on a single flint tool, they had a number of different ones, each for doing its own job. Among these were the first true knives, chisels and engraving tools. Even more important, they made tools of new materials; bone, ivory and reindeer antler. The bone tools included awls for boring holes, and delicately-eyed needles for stitching skins.

The same period saw the invention of three new weapons: the harpoon for spearing fish; the spear-thrower; and perhaps the bow and arrow. The illustrations opposite show (1) a barbed harpoon head, (2) a spear-thrower, together with a drawing of it in use, (3) a Stone Age rock-painting in Spain, probably of later date, which depicts men hunting with bows and arrows. With these long-distance weapons and the methods of collective hunting of which we have evidence – for example, driving animals over cliffs – these men must have been very similar to the hunting peoples who inhabit some parts of the world today.

In Britain men of the late Old Stone Age lived wherever possible in the mouths of caves, like those of the Cheddar Gorge in Somerset, Creswell Crags in Derbyshire, and Kent's Cavern in Devon. Many different types of implements have been excavated from the floors of these caves, including bone sewing-needles, bone harpoons, and a wide range of stone implements. Other objects excavated from British caves are illustrated on the left.

But not everyone lived in caves. In places where caves were few men were now able to survive in the open, despite the severe cold of the last Ice Age.

The so-called mammoth hunters of southern Russia wore leather clothes. For shelter they built tents of animal skins, supported by poles and held down at the edges by mammoth tusks and heavy stones. We know from excavations that the dwellings were oval in shape, with floors sunk into the ground;

he 'roofs' must have been fairly high, for a fire was kept burning inside. This was an early ancestor of the modern house.

Strong feelings

We began this chapter by suggesting that one important way in which human beings differ from the lower animals is that they have the power of thought. By thought, Stone Age man was gradually finding out how to manage and control some of the forces of nature. Without the leather clothes, the huts, fire, his hunting implements, nature would have finished off the mammoth-hunters of southern Russia in no time at all. They could not have survived the cold for one night without the things that man had invented.

Nevertheless, it would be wrong to suppose that it is the power of thought alone which makes human beings different from animals. Men display a characteristic concern for their dead, and people of the late Old Stone Age were deeply moved by the loss of their kith and kin. They buried them with care, placing in the grave food, tools and other needful things. Perhaps the belief had already grown up that the dead were not dead at all but had passed on to another world.

It seems likely that men of this time had strong religious feelings. They may have worshipped a mother goddess, whom they believed made all nature rich and fertile. Little statues of such a figure are often found in their caves and encampments.

Cave art

But the most striking proof that these early modern men were men of feeling is in the wonder and beauty of their art.

One day in 1879 a Spanish nobleman was digging into the floor of a cave at Altamira in Spain. He knew that Old Stone Age people had lived there, so he was digging to see if he could find any flint or bone tools. The nobleman's young daughter was with him, but she had wandered off on her own. Suddenly, the little girl's voice rang out through the gloom. 'Toros! Toros!' ('Bulls! Bulls!') she shouted. As her father ran towards her, he could see that she was pointing excitedly at the ceiling. And no wonder! Stretching in a long line right across it was painted a procession of huge bison bulls. This was how the first cave painting was discovered, after no human eye had looked at it for perhaps 10,000 years.

Since then, many other painted caves have been found in southern France and northern Spain. The most famous of them all, at Lascaux, was discovered by four schoolboys in 1940.

Mother goddess of the late Old Stone Age, from Czechoslovakia.

Opposite page

Above: bison bull at Altamira. Paintings were sometimes superimposed on one another. Like the cave painting on page 16, this is a drawing.

Below: photograph of a group of wild horses at Lascaux. On the right is part of a bison.

22

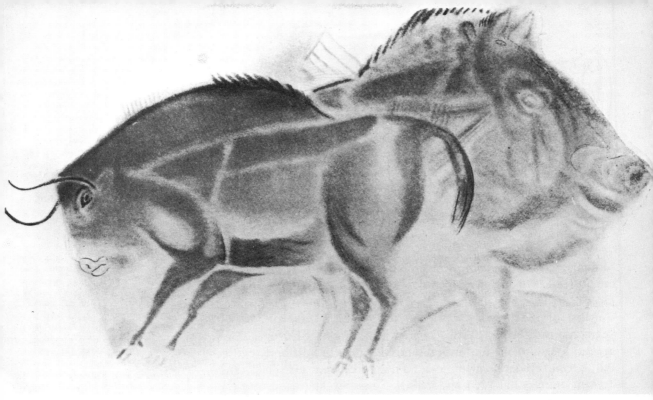

Drawing from a cave painting showing a bison, his side struck by three arrows.

Similar pictures are to be seen in eastern Spain and north Africa, but instead of being in caverns, these are out in the open, on the faces of rocks.

Most of the pictures were made between 30,000 and 10,000 years ago, while the ice still covered large tracts of Europe. They are of the animals that were hunted: bison, wild horse, cattle, red deer, reindeer, mammoth. They are coloured black and brown, orange, light red and yellow. Some are engraved into the rock, while others are cut in such deep relief that they are almost carvings or sculptures.

To make them, the artists used a wide range of tools: flint chisels, awls, knives and scrapers. They probably had crayons also, made brushes by chewing the ends of sticks, and used pads of moss or fur to put on the big colour washes. For mixing the colours the shoulder-blades of animals served as palettes. To enable them to see in the darkness, the artists used tiny lamps in which they burned fat or blubber. These are the oldest lamps yet discovered.

Why were the cave paintings made? No one knows. They were not simply wall decorations, for often they are not in the parts of the caves where the hunters themselves lived. This was near the entrance, so that light could enter and the smoke escape. But many paintings are in places that are difficult to reach; at the heart of the caves, beyond dangerous waterfalls and chasms.

Most people think that the pictures were made in connexion with some form of magic rite. Arrows are sometimes scored on the sides of the animals, so maybe the drawings were meant to bring success in the chase. As the artist-magician killed the animal on the wall of the cave, so would the tribe in the real hunting which followed.

Magician. He wears the skin of an animal and a mask surmounted by deer antlers. He seems to be dancing, perhaps in connexion with a magic ritual. This and the bison are from the cave of 'Les Trois Frères', France.

24

Top: horse, carved in mammoth ivory; *bottom:* pebble engraved with the figure of a deer. *Right:* head of a woman. With its elaborate hair-style and sensitive features, this seems to be the earliest known attempt at making a human portrait.

With the growth of rituals of this kind, it is possible that the arts of dancing and music-making had their beginning. But such practices would have left little trace. Only the paintings have miraculously survived. They are a remarkable heritage.

Besides their paintings, the early artists made little statuettes of animals. One of the masterpieces of Old Stone Age art is the sculpture of a horse which is only about three inches long and has been carved out of mammoth ivory. We have already mentioned the 'goddess' figures; and occasionally they made portraits of each other. Nor could they resist decorating their tools and weapons. The harpoon head and the spear-thrower illustrated on page 16 are examples of this work. They also made necklets, bracelets and headgear to decorate themselves.

So the first people who unquestionably belong to the family of modern man were not only skilful tool-makers and hunters; they were highly gifted artists.

Dates to remember

from 2,000,000 to 500,000 years ago	Southern ape-man
about 500,000 years ago	Erect man
about 250,000 years ago	Swanscombe man
about 35,000 years ago	Modern man in Europe
30,000 to 10,000 years ago	The making of the cave paintings

Things to do

1 Much of the story told in this book depends on archaeological evidence. Find out as much as you can about how the archaeologist works. In particular, find out about the main methods of dating excavated objects: (a) dating by layer, (b) pollen dating, (c) radio-carbon dating. Useful books are listed below.

2 See if there are any archaeological excavations at present going on in your own area; and, if possible, pay a visit to one. Your local museum should be able to help with information.

3 Start a collection of newspaper cuttings relating to archaeological discoveries.

4 Make a list of five substances in use today that could be expected to survive if buried for 100,000 years. Make a second list of five substances which would rot away.

5 Using the picture of Peking man, as well as the information about him, describe an imaginary day in his life.

6 Find out all you can about the life of one of the primitive peoples who have continued to live a Stone Age existence down to the present day. (There are often good T.V. programmes on the life of primitive peoples.)

7 Prepare a list of all the inventions made in the Old Stone Age. Then list some of the outstanding inventions of the last hundred years. Which series of inventions do you consider the most important? Explain why.

8 One important type of Old Stone Age man, Neanderthal man, has not been discussed in this chapter. He lived from about 100,000 to 35,000 years ago, but is not thought to have been a direct ancestor of modern man. Find out more about Neanderthal man and say why you think he died out.

Books to read

Liam de Paor, *Archaeology*, Penguin
E. Pyddoke, *What is Archaeology?* John Baker
Leonard Woolley, *The Young Archaeologist*, Nelson

Right: evolution of man during the Ice Ages, showing the relative size of the brain in Southern ape-man, Erect man and Modern man. No drawing of the facial features of Swanscombe man can be given, since only three bones from the back of the skull have been found.

Besides archaeology, another way of finding out about prehistory is by studying the habits of primitive peoples still living in parts of Africa, South America and Australia. This photograph shows an Australian aborigine cutting a tree with a stone implement.

years ago	
3,400,000,000	oldest known rocks
1,600,000,000	first fossils
200,000,000	first mammals
20,000,000	man's ancestors separate from those of the ape
2,000,000	southern ape-man
600,000	

ice-age

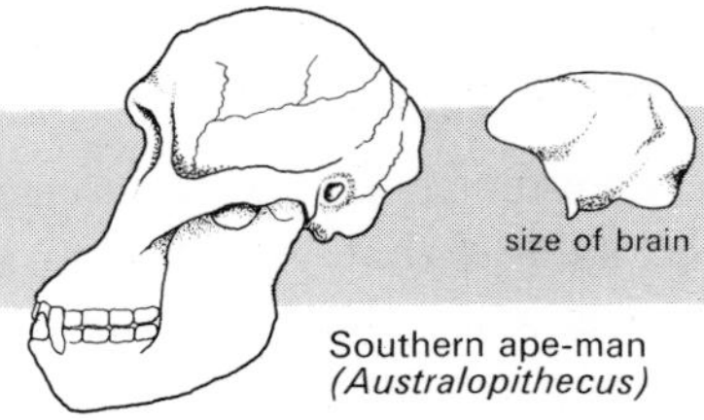

size of brain

Southern ape-man dying out
Erect man

Southern ape-man
(Australopithecus)

500,000

ice age

size of brain

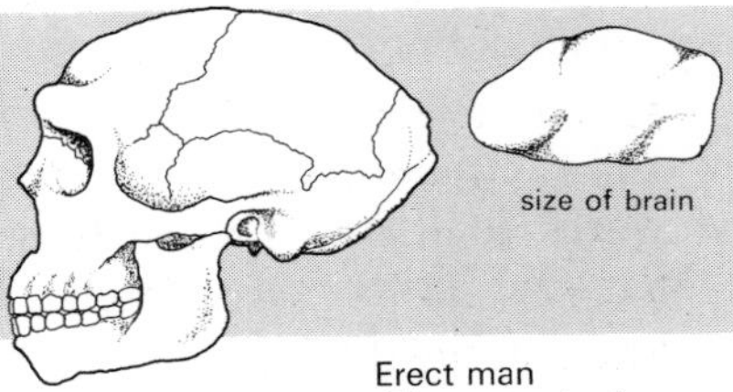

400,000

African hand-axes
yew spear, Clacton-on-Sea

Erect man
(Homo erectus)

300,000

Swanscombe man

ice age

200,000

100,000 ice age

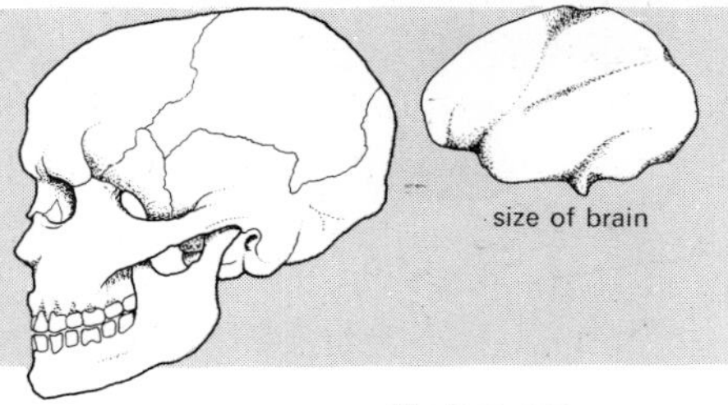

size of brain

30,000 Modern man in Europe
10,000 period of cave art

today

Modern man
(Homo sapiens)

Chapter 2
The first farmers

Different races, different paces

In chapter 1 we were concerned with the Old Stone Age. Throughout that long period man was a hunter. In this chapter we deal with the New Stone Age, when for the first time man became a farmer.

However, the beginning of farming and, with it, of the New Stone Age, did not come at the same time everywhere.

Ten thousand years ago, with the final retreat of the ice back towards the poles, men had found their way into most parts of the world that are now inhabited. Gradually the various races of mankind came into being. There were three main racial groups: the Negroes of central Africa, with their dark skins and dark, tightly curled hair; the white Caucasoid races of Europe, the Near East and north Africa; and finally, the yellow-skinned

The chief races of mankind (in ancient times), except for Bushmen, and Australian and Pacific peoples. The arrow shows the route of the Mongoloids.

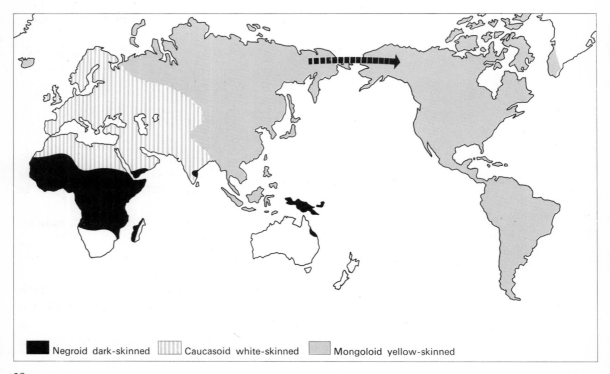

Negroid dark-skinned   Caucasoid white-skinned   Mongoloid yellow-skinned

Mongoloids who occupied most of Asia. This last race had also settled in America. During the Ice Ages, with so much water locked up at the North Pole, sea-levels were lower than they are today; and in consequence there was a land-bridge joining Siberia to Alaska. Using this bridge, groups of Mongoloids crossed over from Asia and gradually colonized the whole American continent. But with the melting of the ice, sea-levels rose again, submerging the land-bridge, so that Asia and America were separated. It was in this way that the 'Indians' of the New World became cut off from the people of the Old World until Columbus 'discovered' them less than 500 years ago.

But we must return to prehistoric times. Since the different races of mankind were scattered, advances made in one part of the world might take thousands of years to reach another. This was the case with farming.

There were already many farming villages among the white peoples of the Near East by 7000 B.C. (i.e., 7,000 years before the birth of Christ). But elsewhere, completely ignorant of this new way of life, the majority of men continued to live much as they had done in the Old Stone Age. The inhabitants of northern Europe (including Britain) remained hunters for many more centuries. Some peoples of Negro and Mongol blood lagged even further behind. Thus, the New Stone Age which started about 8000 B.C. in the Near East, did not begin in northern Europe until after 4000 B.C. In other places it began still later, while, in a sense, certain isolated tribes of primitive hunters have not entered the New Stone Age to the present day.

The invention of farming

Where, when, and how did man first become a farmer?

There are two sides to farming: first, the keeping of domestic animals, and second, the growing of crops. For the hunter to become a farmer, therefore, two different advances had to be made:

1 Man had to tame or domesticate certain of the wild animals which previously had been hunted.
2 He had to learn how to till the soil, and how to sow, cultivate and harvest wheat, barley and other crops.

Both these developments seem to have occurred alongside each other, so that the first farmers practised from the start what is today known as 'mixed farming'. Of course, the changeover from hunting was an extremely gradual process. For a long while the pioneer farmers still had to hunt as well.

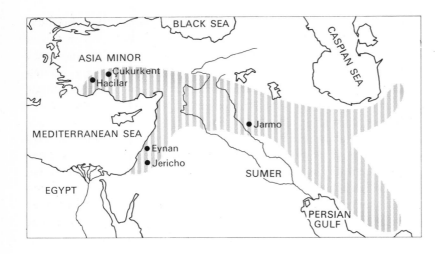

Early farming in south-west Asia. Archaeologists now excavating in Turkey are finding more New Stone Age villages, and this area could perhaps be extended.

The domestication of animals

The area over which archaeologists have discovered the remains of the world's earliest farmers has been shaded on the map. This zone covers a wide arc in south-western Asia. Beginning with Palestine and southern Turkey, it runs eastwards to the Caspian Sea and then swings sharply down to the Persian Gulf. All over this area the bones of domesticated goats, cattle, pigs and sheep have been found in excavations. They had been buried some time between 8000 B.C. and 5000 B.C., and are the remains of the earliest farm animals that are known.

One great advantage of herding animals instead of hunting them will be obvious. Hunting is a chancy business: you can hunt for days and catch nothing. Herded animals, on the other hand, can be immediately killed, so your food supply is certain.

But herding had a second important advantage. Unlike the hunter, the farmer can make use of the living as well as the dead animal. A dead animal cannot be milked, and neither can a wild one; but tame animals can. Similarly, it is only from tame animals that, year after year, you can take a fleece of wool. The taming of the common farmyard animals, therefore, made available several things which were out of the question before, yet which have been considered 'necessities' ever since. By hunting, man had long known how to obtain meat and skins; stock-breeding enabled him to get these more easily and in addition provided him with regular supplies of wool, milk, butter and cheese.

Clearly, then, the domestication of animals was a great step forward. But although we know roughly where and when this took place, no one can say for certain how it was done.

The dog was the first animal of all to be tamed. Probably he is descended from a now extinct type of jackal, and had begun to live with man in the hunting stage, when he would be attracted by the bones and scraps that were always available near human encampments. Gradually a bond of affection grew up between the four-legged scrounger and his master: and the dog became man's faithful helpmate and companion.

But if the dog volunteered to live with man, the first farm animals had to be forcibly captured. Archaeologists have noticed that the skeletons of early domesticated beasts are always extremely small. So they think that the farmers may have captured young animals from the wild herds, purposely choosing ones which were weak and undersized. Not only would these be easier to catch, they would be far easier to handle in captivity.

The cultivation of crops

The harvesting of wheat and barley developed over the same area where farm animals were domesticated; and it developed during the same period, between 8000 and 5000 B.C.

How is this known? It is because of the things archaeologists have excavated. Flint sickles have been found at many places. Usually these have flint blades set in handles of wood or, as in the illustration *(left)*, of antler. Elsewhere, querns for grinding corn into flour by rubbing have been discovered. The illustration below shows what a quern of this period looked like and how it was used. Because of its shape and the way it became hollowed in the middle, archaeologists call it a 'saddle' quern. Sometimes

Above: New Stone Age sickle with flint teeth, excavated at Mount Carmel in Palestine. The top of the antler handle is decorated with an animal's head, perhaps of a goat.

Grinding corn in a 'saddle' quern at Jericho. As the woman grinds the corn the flour falls into a dish. It was laborious, time-consuming work.

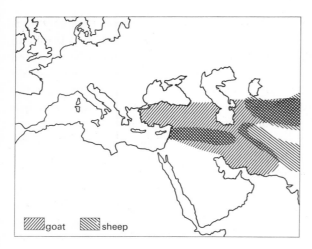
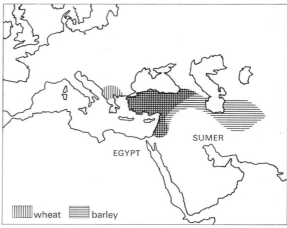

goat sheep

wheat barley

SUMER

EGYPT

pits for storing grain are found and primitive ovens for the baking of bread. At first, only flat, unleavened bread could be made, for yeast was unknown.

However, the 'sickles', querns and other objects we have mentioned do not necessarily mean that men were growing cultivated crops. Such things would be required if wild cereals were being gathered. Indeed, there must have been a stage when only wild crops were gathered. Man reaped before he sowed. But at many places flint hoes have been discovered, and these are proof that patches of ground were being cleared and cultivated.

At Jarmo actual wheat and barley dating from about 5000 B.C. were excavated. These early grains of corn were not the same as the wild varieties, either. Scientists say that they had definitely been improved by careful cultivation.

But why was farming developed in the south-western corner of Asia, and not somewhere else? It is because this particular area is the only part of the Old World where the wild ancestors of sheep, pigs and cattle, as well as of wheat and barley, were to be found. (See the maps above.) The wild wheat and barley from which our modern grains are descended still grow over this region even today.

By 3000 B.C., as we shall see later, great civilizations flourished in the river valleys of Sumer and Egypt. Because these were the earliest civilizations, it was originally thought that the art of farming must have been discovered in these countries also. But we now know that this is untrue. In fact farming could not have been discovered in Sumer or Egypt, simply because the necessary wild plants and animals were not available. For instance, in neither

Left: distribution of wild sheep and wild goats. Wild pig and cattle could be found throughout south-west Asia. North Africa (including Egypt) had the wild cow, but not the wild pig. *Right:* distribution of wild wheat and barley.

Wild ancestors of wheat *(left),* barley *(right).* Try to find pictures or actual ears of present-day barley and wheat and see how they compare.

country did wheat or barley grow of its own accord (see map). If there was to be corn in Sumer and Egypt, man had to take it there himself, and before this happened, farming had to be developed in the area we are discussing. For only here were all the necessary things to be found.

The first villages

The coming of farming was not the only important advance made in this region.

As a hunter man had no settled home, but wandered over wide tracts of country. Often the roof over his head was the roof of a cave, or else he contented himself with a tent or some other temporary shelter. But once man began to farm, there were great advantages in settling in one spot. Before the land could be sown, it had to be cleared of trees and other wild plants. Fields had to be banked and folds constructed for the keeping of cattle. Then the farmer would want to build himself a real house. There was little point in starting from scratch, year after year, in different places. It was better to pick one place and settle there permanently. When a number of farming families live permanently together in one place, we call it a village. It is hardly surprising, then, that the area where farming began was also the area of the world's oldest villages.

Harvesting outside Jericho in about 7000 B.C. The town wall is on the left. The man nearest to us is using a sickle to cut the corn. What are the trees in the centre of the drawing and what type of domesticated animal is grazing beneath them?

Jericho

Archaeologists have discovered early villages in Persia, Iraq, Syria, Turkey, Cyprus, Jordan and Palestine. Two of the oldest are Jericho and Eynan. Both are in Palestine and date from before 7000 B.C. By this time, indeed, Jericho had become a small town. The site had certainly been well chosen. It stood in an oasis, watered by a spring which still produces 1,000 gallons of water per minute.

Nine thousand years ago Jericho's inhabitants lived in small round or oval houses which had domed roofs, so that they looked rather like the traditional beehive. These houses had from one to three rooms, and were built of sun-baked brick, with plastered mud floors. Primitive though they seem to us, they provided the most lavish living accommodation so far known.

We read of the walls of Jericho in the Bible. But not many people know that the first wall had already been built before 7000 B.C. It enclosed the whole town area of about nine acres, and was a massive stone wall, with great round towers set along it at regular intervals. The towers had inner stairways so that guards could mount safely to the top.

Outside the wall there was a ditch, twenty-five feet wide and

Above: the great wall of Jericho. Archaeologists cut a 'section' at right angles across the defences of the early town. The man second from top is standing on one of the round towers; the man in the foreground is at the bottom of the rock-cut ditch.

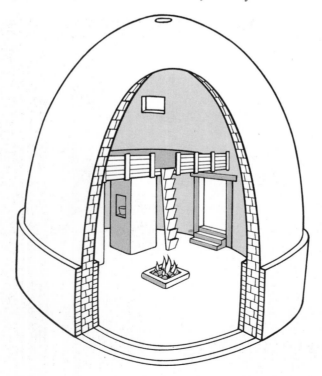

Diagram of a domed house at Khirokitia, Cyprus. Khirokitia, built about 5500 B.C., was a later town than Jericho, but was of the same stage in man's development and its houses were similar. An unusual feature of some of the Khirokitia houses was a partial upper floor supported on two limestone pillars. Note the tiny window.

six feet deep. An amazing thing about this ditch is that it is cut into solid rock. Yet the only tool the Jericho people used was probably a stone pounder. The making of the town defences must have been a tremendous undertaking. We may be sure that many hundreds of inhabitants co-operated in the work. We may also be sure that some kind of town government would have been needed to plan and carry through such an ambitious operation.

Owing to the strange burial customs of the Jericho people, actual portraits of a few inhabitants of the oldest town have survived. At death their heads were cut off and buried separately. Before burial, however, the skulls were covered with clay, the eyes inlaid with shells, and the whole head shaped to look like the dead person. Some of the faces are finely modelled and seem very lifelike. Historians think that this strange practice may be connected with the religion of the Jericho people.

But we know little about religious matters at this time. The only thing we can be sure of is that all over the farming area some form of goddess was worshipped, for little clay or stone statues of her are found in almost every village. Probably she was a fertility goddess and was worshipped because she made the crops grow and the herds increase.

Above: Goddess figure. This one was excavated at Cukurkent, an early farming village in southern Turkey. It is carved in a hard brown stone and stands less than 2 inches high. Compare with the illustration on page 18.

Portrait head from Jericho. The clay has flaked off in places, revealing the skull beneath.

New crafts

In addition to being centres of farming, the first villages were also places where several important new crafts were developed.

Perhaps the oldest of these was basket-work. Imprints or impressions of coiled rush mats have been found on some of the floors at Jericho. The mats themselves have rotted away, but had they survived they would have been over 8,000 years old. The methods of basket-work and mat-making invented in the New Stone Age have hardly changed from that time to this.

A second craft, weaving, probably grew out of basket-work. It is really much the same, except that basketry is made from natural straw and withies, while weaving is done with threads of wool, flax or cotton. Such thread had first to be twisted or spun.

Spinning was done in the New Stone Age by the twirling of a spindle suspended from the hand. Spindles were made of wood, and so have not survived, but disc-shaped spinning whorls made of clay or stone are often found. They have a hole in them through which the spindle fitted. The idea of weighting the spindle in this way was to keep it rotating for a longer period. Wool and flax must have been the earliest threads to be spun; flax seeds have been found at Jarmo and other farming villages. Cotton did not grow in south-western Asia, and was introduced from India at a much later date.

The looms used for weaving were simple affairs, consisting of two wooden rods pegged into the ground, with the warp threads stretched tightly between them. The earliest known piece of cloth comes from southern Turkey: it is probably of wool and was made over 8,000 years ago.

Basket-work, spinning and weaving may have been invented by women and it is possible that women also made the first pottery.

This important new craft was discovered hundreds of years after the beginning of farming, probably somewhere in southern Asia Minor. But the making of pottery vessels quickly spread throughout the farming region. Clay changes into pottery when it is heated, so perhaps the first discoveries were made accidentally: if a fire was lit on a clay-daubed hearth, next morning it might be found that some of the clay had hardened into pottery.

At first housewives may have made pots in their spare time. The earliest ones were very crude, and usually undecorated. But by 5000 B.C., in some places, there were highly skilled male potters at work. They had to manage without the potter's wheel, so they built up the sides of their vessels by winding round a continuous roll of clay. After this, with one hand inside the pot and the other

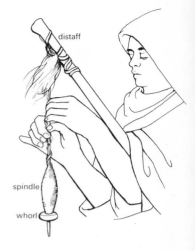

How spinning was probably carried out in the New Stone Age.

An early loom, from a drawing on an Egyptian pottery dish of about 4400 B.C.

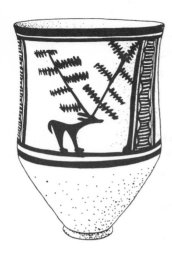

Pot from Iran, made about 4000 B.C. What kind of animal is depicted? Why has the potter exaggerated its antlers?

outside, they thinned its walls and perfected the shape. Then they decorated, painted, and glazed the pot – techniques which had only recently been invented. Originally pottery had been fired in an open fire, but by 5000 B.C. a closed kiln was used.

In the beauty of its shape, its lovely colours and varied designs, some of this New Stone Age pottery is as fine as any that has been made since. Certainly it is far more attractive than most of the crockery we have in our own homes. Man's artistic gifts, which had first developed in the Old Stone Age, had not left him. He made tools and built houses and tamed animals because these were useful things to do. He lavished much skill on the decoration of his pottery because he liked to have about him bright and attractive things.

Alongside the new crafts, the first farmers improved their ability to work in stone: that is why this period is known as the New Stone Age. In place of the Old Stone Age hand-axe, we find a skilfully ground and polished axe-head which could be hafted and possessed a hard, sharp cutting edge (see page 171). Bowls, dishes and vases were also cut from stone, then decorated and burnished. At some places stone vessels were preferred to pottery ones, perhaps because they were less easily broken. But they were not so easily made, for the shapes had to be patiently chipped and ground out, which must have been a long and wearisome operation.

Stone belonged to the age which was passing. But another material was coming into use. Already men were beginning to work with metal. The metal was copper which occurs, not only as

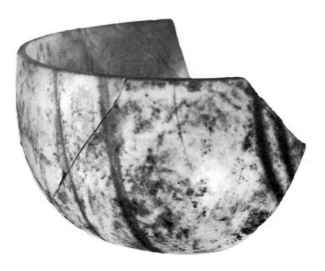

Limestone bowl excavated at Jarmo.

ore, but sometimes as pure metal. At first, bits of this natural metal were hammered to make small objects like pins and beads. To do this the copper would be heated, probably in a pottery oven. But a way of making fire sufficiently hot to smelt the ore and produce molten copper had not yet been discovered.

Still, a great future was being opened up by these early experiments in metalwork. Soon bronze (a mixture of copper and a little tin) was to become so important for the making of tools and weapons that archaeologists have named the period following the New Stone Age after this metal.

Towards civilization

The foundations of civilization were laid by the first farmers and craftsmen of south-western Asia. Civilization has been called 'the art of living in cities'. In the New Stone Age, there were no great cities. Jericho was large for that time, yet it was only a small town. Life was still very plain and simple. Small shrines had been built, but there were no fine temples. Some towns and villages may have had a local ruler or chieftain, but powerful kings were unknown. Nothing had happened to weld the inhabitants of a wide area into a single united people. At this time there were no nations or empires. Writing had not been invented, so we are still in prehistoric times.

Man did not become fully civilized in the New Stone Age. Yet, before the first cities could be made, and with them the earliest civilizations, people had to learn how to farm the land, and live the simple life of a farming village. This was the great step forward taken in the New Stone Age.

If the time we have now reached is 5000 B.C., the world's first cities had to wait another 1,500 years. When they came, they were built, not in the area we have been speaking of in this chapter, but in Mesopotamia.

Dates to remember

8000 B.C.   End of the last Ice Age
8000 B.C.   Beginning of the New Stone Age in the Near East
4000 B.C.   Beginning of the New Stone Age in northern Europe

Things to do

1   Make a list of some of the things that are still obtained by hunting. Could any of the animals concerned be domesticated? Why have they not been?

2   By visiting your local museum, or by referring to books (see also chapter 10 of this one), make drawings of some of the things that date from the New Stone Age in Britain. Compare these to the illustrations found in this chapter. Why is it that the British things are so much later in date than similar objects that have been found in the Near East?

3   Find a picture of a woman spinning in the Middle Ages, before the invention of the spinning wheel. Copy it. Is this basically the same method of spinning as that used in the New Stone Age? (See page 32).

4   Although the practice of farming spread to us from south-west Asia, there was at least one part of the world where it was invented independently. From reference books, find out what you can about the discovery of farming in Mexico. Were the same crops sown and the same animals domesticated?

Books to read

I. Doncaster, *Life in Prehistoric Times*, Longmans

S. Cole, *The Neolithic Revolution*, British Museum

M. and C. H. B. Quennell, *Everyday Life in Prehistoric Times*, Batsford

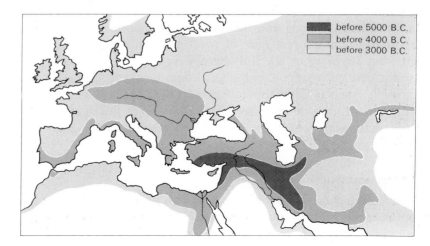

before 5000 B.C.
before 4000 B.C.
before 3000 B.C.

Spread of farming and the New Stone Age.

Chapter 3
The first cities: Sumer

The beginnings of Sumer

Mesopotamia is the country which lies between the river Tigris in the east and the river Euphrates in the west. The name actually means 'the land between the two rivers'. Since these rivers flow through south-western Asia for over a thousand miles, Mesopotamia is a very long, narrow land. But it is only the southern part which concerns us here, the part that lies immediately to the north of the Persian Gulf. This is the place where our civilization was born. In ancient times it was known as Sumer.

About 9,000 years ago when Jericho, the oldest town, was flourishing, most of what later became Sumer was still below the waters of the Persian Gulf. For many centuries, however, the waters of the Tigris and the Euphrates had been carrying down large quantities of silt from the mountains of the north and as a result of this deposition the sea-bed was gradually being raised higher and higher. By 5000 B.C. some of it at least had become dry land.

Before another thousand years had passed men had begun to inhabit this new land. They came from the Iranian Plateau, to the east of the Tigris: part of the zone, where, as we have seen, the art of farming and village life had already been discovered. They brought with them not only a knowledge of how to farm, but also seed corn, cattle and sheep.

Finding a place to settle was not easy. Much of the land was covered with swamps and marshes, full of tall reeds. Elsewhere, by contrast, mile upon mile of parched earth seemed useless for growing anything at all. But there were other places where luxuriant date palms grew and where conditions were just right for farming. At such places the settlers built their first villages, making huts out of the reeds. They tilled their small fields with stone hoes, cultivating wheat and barley, and keeping cattle, goats and sheep.

Earth and water

The country they had come to was one of great disadvantages, but also of great promise. The small patches of ground which could be farmed proved to be richer and more fertile than any

Limestone head of a typical Sumerian.

The main Sumerian cities in the Bronze Age.

man had cultivated before. The whole of Sumer was covered with this same rich earth. It was the silt or alluvium which the rivers had spread over the entire valley in the process of lifting it out of the sea.

The earth itself then was full of promise. The main difficulty was over water. Hardly any rain fell in Mesopotamia, so away from the rivers the soil was too dry for farming. On the other hand, every year the rivers flooded, which meant that close to them most of the land was permanent swamp. In some places there was too little water; in others too much.

The Sumerians develop irrigation

Supposing, though, that the rivers and floods could be controlled. Supposing the swamps could be drained, and the dry places watered. Then the whole plain would become rich and fertile.

In the highlands, the ancestors of the Sumerians had learned how to tame wild animals; now, in this new land, if progress was to be made, the Sumerians had to tame a great river. This they did with the Euphrates. First they built huge banks on either side of the river so that, even at flood time, it could be contained within its own bed. Then they constructed complicated systems of canals and dykes, reservoirs and dams, by which means the water could be distributed wherever and whenever it was wanted.

Controlling the distribution of water in this way is called irrigation. It was the Sumerians who first practised it on a large scale.

Civilization becomes possible

An irrigation system could not be built by small groups of men. If wide areas were to be cultivated, water had to be carried far inland. To do this the people of a whole district would have had to work together. A great deal of hard labour was necessary. But there had to be careful organization too. The whole scheme had to be planned, ordered and directed.

Even when the irrigation works had been completed, careful planning and control would still be needed. The dykes and banks had to be maintained in good repair. Canals had to be kept clean, otherwise they would quickly become choked with silt. Then it was necessary for somebody to see that the water was fairly distributed; that every farmer received an adequate supply; that one man did not steal the water of another. This meant that each district needed a strong permanent government which everybody served and obeyed.

Hundreds of people had combined together before – in building the walls of Jericho, for instance. But in Sumer, because of the need to control and distribute the waters, thousands became united. Thousands of men living and co-operating together could make, not a village or a town merely, but a city. So it was that, for the first time in history, civilization – the art of living in cities – became possible.

Sumerian lady engaged in worship. This statuette is from Lagash and dates from about 2900 B.C.

Shortage of materials

However, before cities could be built and civilization develop, the Sumerians had another difficulty to overcome. Many of the raw materials necessary for civilized life were not to be found in Mesopotamia. Indeed, many of the materials necessary for successful farming were not there either. There were no metals, flints, or building-stone, and – apart from the palm – no timber.

But again the Sumerians responded to this challenge and found a solution. They began to import all the things they needed from abroad. They brought timber from the mountains in the north-east and from Syria. Stone and copper came from Oman on the Persian Gulf. Semi-precious stones, like lapis lazuli, came from Afghanistan. Silver and lead came from the Taurus mountains. Tin was brought from as far north as Asia Minor or even Europe.

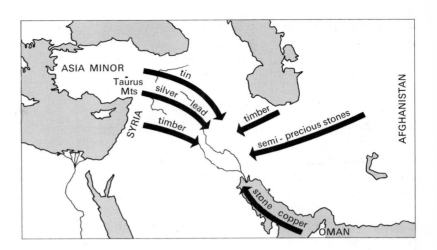

Sumerian trade.

These things were imported by land and sea. Above all, from the earliest times, large quantities of goods travelled backwards and forwards along the Tigris and Euphrates. The ancient name of the Euphrates was Urudu, meaning 'the copper river'; which tells us that copper was one of the chief imported commodities coming into Sumer.

The Sumerians had no money. But their farming was so efficient by this time that the land was producing far more than the inhabitants actually needed for themselves. So they were able to trade by barter, exchanging their own surplus of corn and dates, leather, wool and pottery for the things they needed. Thus trade developed on a scale which had never been known before.

The first cities

So determined and energetic were these Sumerians that by 3500 B.C. they had triumphed over their difficulties, and there had arisen in the land the earliest cities: Ur, Erech, Eridu, Lagash, Nippur.

It was irrigation which had made these cities possible. Each stood at the centre of its own irrigation district, surrounded by many miles of rich and fertile farmlands.

Improvements in agriculture

In the course of this great advance from village life to the building of cities, the Sumerians made a whole series of important inventions and discoveries. Most of these are still benefiting us today.

They made great advances in agriculture. They began to use an

43

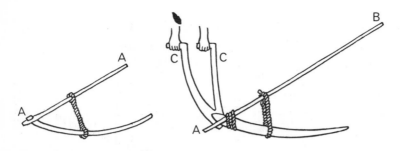

How the hoe may have developed into the plough. Compare these drawings with the models of an Egyptian hoe and plough illustrated on page 73.

ox-drawn plough. The illustration shows how this idea may have been developed, by extending the handle of the hoe (A-A) so that it became the plough beam (A-B). Upright handles (C, C) would then be added to enable the ploughman to guide the plough. At first, instead of the oxen being yoked, the plough beam had to be fastened to their horns by means of ropes.

Using the plough, much larger areas could be cultivated than before. With only the hand hoe, food growing must have been more like gardening than anything else, but agriculture could now be practised on a much more effective scale.

This invention is important for another reason. By harnessing the oxen, man was using and controlling a source of energy other than his own. In a sense, therefore, the 'beast of burden' was really the first step towards all our other means of power: water and wind power, the steam-engine, the petrol motor, even the atomic generator. But apart from this, everyone knows how important animal power itself has been in the past – and still is in many countries.

A two-wheeled chariot. This relief carving from Ur shows one of the earliest detailed representations of the wheel. Make a drawing of it and label the hub, one of the joining devices, and the leather tyre. How does the chariot differ from those shown on the 'Royal Standard' (page 52), which is from the same period (2900–2400 B.C.)?

Ploughing was not the only purpose for which draught oxen were used in ancient Mesopotamia. The Sumerians adopted wheeled transport. Their earliest wheel (see page 40) consisted of three pieces of solid wood joined together and bound with leather tyres. The wheels turned in one piece with the axles, which were simply tied under the cart by leather thongs. Now oxen could be made to draw a farm cart. Wheeled vehicles were employed also for general transport; and the Sumerians soon had war chariots. Vehicles were drawn by asses, as well as oxen, but the horse had not yet been introduced.

Another extremely ingenious invention of the Sumerians was the seed drill. The illustration below shows how this machine worked. First it made a groove (or drill) in the soil. Then the seed itself was guided into the drill by means of a funnel and a long thin tube. Finally, the man walking behind covered the seed up.

In all essentials this is our modern method of sowing. But actually we do not owe it to the Sumerians. Somehow the idea of setting seed in rows got lost and forgotten. The method of sowing we read of in the Bible is not the ingenious Sumerian one. Instead, as you will remember from the parable of the sower, the seed was simply scattered from the hand, or sown 'broadcast'. After the Sumerians, all over the world farmers went on sowing their seed in this primitive and wasteful fashion until about 200 years ago. Then in the eighteenth century, an Englishman called Jethro Tull invented what was really the old Sumerian seed drill all over again. (See *A History of Britain*, vol. 3, page 159.) And for a long time people would not use it because they thought it too new-fangled and modern.

The Sumerians, with all their advanced ideas, must have produced bumper harvests of wheat and barley. Moreover, the climate was so favourable that they were able to gather two harvests every year.

Right: Sumerian seed drill. It is drawn by two oxen with their driver by them. Another man is shown walking alongside the drill. He has a hopper or seed-bag strapped over his shoulder, from which he takes handfuls of grain to drop into the funnel. This scene was carved on a small stone cylinder seal. It was rolled over clay, and used to mark personal property or to seal documents *(above)*.

They were successful as pasture farmers too. The fine quality of the Sumerian sheep can be seen by looking at the top illustration on page 52. These deep, heavy fleeces tell us that there must have been a plentiful supply of woollen cloth. At this time sheep were plucked, not shorn.

Finally, we know that the Sumerians had a highly developed dairy industry. Temple decorations which are almost 5,000 years old show the milking of a cow, the straining of milk, and the making of butter.

A Sumerian dairying scene. In the centre are the gates of the cow-yard or dairy. On the right a cow, with her calf in front of her, is being milked. On the left two men strain the milk, while two more are perhaps making butter by rotating their jars.

Specialist craftsmen

Because the Sumerians grew more food than they actually needed, they could obtain large quantities of timber, stone and metal from abroad. But the surplus of food had another important result: it meant that, for the first time, not everyone in the community had to work on the land; some people could become specialist craftsmen.

Originally, in the farming villages of the New Stone Age, each family had done its own craftwork. Pottery, for instance, was made by the women of the house in their spare time. But now, in Sumer, it was no longer necessary for the farmer's wife to make her own pots. The farmer could take some of his surplus corn into the city, and exchange it with a potter for the cooking vessels, bowls and dishes his wife required. In the same way, the farmer himself did not have to make his own flint sickles. He could barter surplus meat or corn with a metal-smith for finely-wrought bronze tools.

Just as the farmer was able to stop doing craftwork, so the potters and the metal-smiths could forget altogether about farming, and work full-time at their own trades. For there would always be farmers able and willing to give them corn and meat in return for the various things they had made.

People who spend all their time, and concentrate all their thought and energy, on doing one job usually become far more skilful and efficient than part-time workers. It is no wonder that these specialist Sumerian craftsmen were soon turning out work that was better than had been done before. It is no wonder either that, like the farmers, they were soon employing new ideas and techniques.

By 3000 B.C., the full-time potters of Sumer were no longer building up their vessels slowly and by hand as part-time potters had always done. They were 'throwing' their pots on the potter's wheel.

Similarly, metal-workers made great advances in their trade. Better types of kilns were introduced which enabled the smith to reduce his copper to a molten state. By adding about 10 per cent of tin to the copper he discovered bronze. He learned the arts of casting, riveting and soldering. Soon, throughout Sumer, tools and weapons of bronze began to replace the old-fashioned stone and copper ones.

This is why the period when the first civilizations developed is known as the Bronze Age. But, again, it has to be remembered that the use of bronze spread very slowly to other parts of the world (some it did not reach until modern times), and it did not always take civilization with it.

In Sumer copper, tin and bronze were not the only known metals. Lead was used; so too were gold and silver, for ceremonial weapons, ornaments and vessels. A vast hoard of metal

Sumerian metal-smiths depicted on a tablet of green stone (about 2900 B.C.). An overseer inspects three craftsmen at a kind of anvil. The picture-writing on the right has not yet been deciphered; it is similar to that of the Kish tablet (page 46).

Right: a goat standing on its
hind legs to sniff the flowers
of a tree. The tree is made
of gold leaf, as is the goat's
face and legs. The body fleece
is of white shell, while the
shoulder fleece, the horns and
eyes are of lapis lazuli.

Below: detail of a golden bull's
head on a harp from Ur,
which dates from about
2750 B.C.

Part of the necklace or head-dress belonging to a queen of Ur. The leaves are of finely beaten gold. This, the bull's head and the goat were all found in the Royal Tombs, Ur, and can be seen today in the British Museum.

objects has been excavated from the royal cemetery at Ur. These show that Sumerian metal-smiths could do almost anything that modern craftsmen can do.

There is not time to discuss all the great inventions that the Sumerians made. But one is so important that we could not possibly leave it out. This is the invention of writing, which was later to spread over the whole world and become the very hall-mark of civilization itself.

It was the priests who invented writing. In order to understand how this happened, we must first find out something about the way the cities of Sumer were governed, and also about Sumerian religion.

Gods, priests and kings

Man, the Sumerians believed, had been created for one purpose: to supply the gods with food, drink and shelter.

Many gods were worshipped in Mesopotamia, but each city had its own particular patron deity, just as different countries today have their patron saints. The chief god of Ur, for instance, was called Nannar.

At the centre of each city there was a great temple, which was thought to be the actual home of the patron god. By building and caring for this temple the citizens provided the god with shelter. How, though, was he to be provided with food and drink? These had to be collected in the form of taxes and offerings.

The Sumerians believed that it was in order to make this system work properly that the god of each city had chosen a king. In addition, each city had many thousands of priests. Generally the king looked after matters of government, making sure that the irrigation system was kept in good repair, that the army was well trained, and so on. Meanwhile, the priests attended to the needs of the god in his temple, for which purpose they collected most of the taxes.

The invention of writing

If a tax collector is to do his job thoroughly, he really needs to keep a record of what he has collected. From about 3500 B.C. this is what the priests of Sumer began to do. At first their records were extremely simple. If so many cattle had been collected they would draw a cow's head, following this with an appropriate number of dots and circles. If so many measures of grain had been brought to the temple, they would draw an ear of corn and then indicate the number as before.

The earliest known example of picture-writing is shown on the right. It is about 5,500 years old, and is a piece of limestone with signs scratched on both sides. The meaning of the pictures on the side which is illustrated seems to be '3 sledges, 2 feet, 1 hand'.

As a rule the priests did not write on stone, but kept their records on tablets of clay. Once baked, however, such tablets were extremely hard, and more or less imperishable. This is fortunate because it means that we are able to follow the various stages through which writing developed. From the simple picture-writing shown on the Kish Tablet, Sumerian writing was gradually improved in two different ways.

In the first place, over the centuries, the method of drawing the pictures was changed. For a stylus (or pen) the Sumerians used a piece of reed with a wedge-shaped end. Working with the point, the early scribes simply scratched a picture of each object into the soft clay.

But this was a slow business. So after a time they began to form their pictures by stamping the stylus. Because of the shape of the stylus, this meant that, from now on, the 'pictures' were built up entirely of wedge-like impressions. It is this fact that gives Sumerian writing its name: cuneiform, meaning 'wedge-shaped'.

As more and more records had to be kept, the scribes wanted to write faster. This led them to simplify their pictures still further, by cutting down the number of stampings and changing their direction, so that they were easier to do. In the end the original objects could hardly be recognized. These developments can be seen by studying the illustration opposite.

Now we come to the second way in which Sumerian writing was improved. Scribes discovered that picture writing had disadvantages. Ideas, thoughts, feelings and actions could not be pictured

The Kish tablet. The sledge may have been used for threshing corn. No one knows for certain what these signs mean.

This diagram shows how the Sumerian scribe held a stylus in one hand and a soft clay tablet in the other. Afterwards the clay was dried. You could make a stylus like this and impress the tip on to clay or another suitable surface to form cuneiform signs.

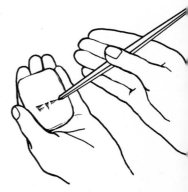

	pictograph	pictograph in the position of cuneiform	early cuneiform	Assyrian
to stand, to go				
fish				
heaven, god				
ox				
grain				

Development of cuneiform.

be - lief

easily. Supposing you wanted to write 'hopeful' or 'hot'. For such words pictures could not be made. At first special signs (called ideographs) were used in these cases. But the trouble was that ideographs were harder to remember than the picture signs (pictographs). And soon there were several thousand of them!

Eventually the Sumerians discovered an ingenious solution to this difficulty. They decided that in future, instead of their signs standing for things and ideas, they would make them stand for *sounds*.

When, for instance, they wanted to write 'belief', they used a sign to represent each of the word's two sounds or syllables.

Under this system   no longer stands for the insect, but only for the sound 'be'. Similarly   does not stand for the thing but for the sound 'leaf'.

This was a great step forward. Before, Sumerian scribes had had to remember a different sign for every single word. But now they had to learn only the basic sounds from which they could build up any word they wanted, syllable by syllable.

The Sumerian language, like every other language, consisted of many hundreds of different syllables. For this reason writing remained a very complicated business and even after the advances we have discussed the scribe still had to memorize about 600 signs. When we learn to write we only have to remember twenty-six. But the Sumerians never realized that all their syllables were made up of various combinations of a few simple sounds. So they never invented an alphabet.

It is not surprising that the cuneiform script remained a complete mystery to the majority of Sumerians. Learning to read and write took many years, and peasant families could not afford to send their children to school; even well-to-do people sent only their sons.

Sumerian schools

Early Sumerian schools were attached to the temples and the teachers were priests. In excavated school buildings of a later date (2000 B.C.), archaeologists have discovered some of the clay tablets on which boys learned to write. On one side of the tablet is the teacher's fair copy of the writing exercise, and on the other side the pupil's attempt – often clumsy and 'ham-fisted' – to imitate it. Exercises were carefully graded, starting with individual signs, then lists of words, and finally full sentences.

Discipline was strict, as is shown by this description of a rather unfortunate day in the life of a Sumerian schoolboy, written about 4,000 years ago:

When I awoke early in the morning I faced my mother and said to her: 'Give me my lunch; I want to go to school.' My mother gave me two rolls and I set out. In the school the man on duty said to me: 'Why are you late?' Afraid, and with my heart pounding, I entered before my teacher and bowed.

King Ur-Nammu paying homage to the Moon god Nannar (See also page 51).

But things went from bad to worse. The boy was whipped because he had 'stared about in the street'; and then because he was 'not properly dressed'. Later came three more doses of the stick: for talking, standing up, and walking outside the gate. Finally the headmaster told him: 'Your writing exercise is not satisfactory', and gave him yet another beating.

As well as learning cuneiform, schoolboys studied religious texts, poetry, and arithmetic.

Sumerian learning

The Sumerians were the first people to devise a system of arithmetic. They could add and subtract, and they also practised multiplication. We are taught to count in 10s and 100s, but the Sumerians counted in 60s. This unit of sixty has been handed down to us, as in the hour and minute, and in our method of dividing the circle into 360 degrees (6 × 60).

The Sumerians had an excellent system of weights and measures. From this comes our pound weight. It is odd to think that when today the butcher weighs out a pound of meat he is

Alabaster statue of a kneeling king or priest, dated about 2750 B.C.

using a weight which was agreed upon over 5,000 years ago in distant Mesopotamia.

But we owe many other things that we take for granted to the Sumerians. It was their priests who worked out the whole basis of our calendar. They decided to measure the year by the moon and this gave them (with some odd days left over) a year of twelve months. Then, because the moon passes through four phases or quarters, they divided the month into four shorter periods. This is the origin of our seven-day week. Incidentally, the interest of the priests in the calendar led to a careful study of the stars, and thus to the beginnings of astronomy.

World literature had its beginning among this people. On their clay tablets they wrote down some of their myths and legends. One of these told how the world was created; another described a great flood, similar to the flood we read of in the Bible. Such floods occurred several times in Sumer when the Euphrates got out of control. The Sumerian flood story was written many hundreds of years before the biblical one; yet it even tells of the building of a great boat, or ark, by Ziusudra, the Sumerian forerunner of Noah, and how:

. . . for seven days and seven nights,
The flood . . . swept over the land,
And the huge boat (was) tossed about by the windstorms on the great
    waters.

Music was another art keenly followed in ancient Sumer. Among the instruments the Sumerians used were clappers, drums, timbrels, harps, lyres, flutes, horns and trumpets.

The city of Ur

Before leaving Sumer, we must say something about one of its greatest cities, Ur. This city was many times larger than the town of Jericho and must have had tens of thousands of inhabitants. Its rampart wall, twenty-five feet high, enclosed an oval-shaped area, three-quarters of a mile long and half a mile wide.

Immediately beyond the west wall was the river Euphrates, and canals ran right round the city on its other sides. These waterways were necessary because Ur depended so much on foreign trade. A north and west harbour provided excellent loading and unloading facilities for the varied and valuable cargoes.

Within the city itself, the most important and impressive place was the temple enclosure, or sacred area. This was really the palace of the Moon god, Nannar, the patron deity of Ur. In its

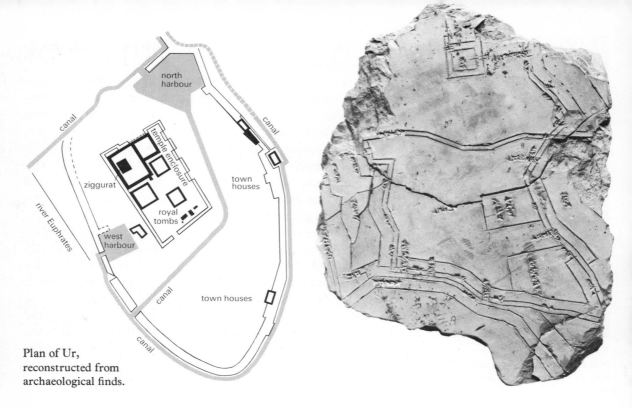

Plan of Ur, reconstructed from archaeological finds.

western corner rose 'the Hill of Heaven', or Ziggurat, a vast tower, built in three stages, on the top of which stood the dwelling place of Nannar himself, the holy of holies.

Below, in the great courtyard, there were other temples, royal tombs, the king's palace, the law court, and many storerooms and administrative offices.

For the most part, the rest of Ur was occupied by the houses of the townsfolk. These were built of brick, and had two or three storeys. The rooms were arranged round a central courtyard, open to the sky. On the ground floor of a typical house there would be a guest room, a kitchen, a lavatory, workrooms and the servants' quarters. A flight of stairs led up to a wooden balcony which ran right round the court, at first-floor level, and so gave access to the living-rooms and bedrooms of the family.

Such houses must have been extremely comfortable to live in. Nor were they the homes of wealthy nobles, but of quite ordinary middle-class people: merchants, shop-keepers, scribes and craftsmen. Sumer – unlike Egypt, which we shall read about in the next chapter – had few rich landowners, but a large middle-class whose prosperity depended mainly on the industry and trade of the cities.

Above: clay tablet showing a map of Nippur, the oldest known city map. It includes important temples, a park, rivers and canals, and the city walls and gates.
Below: reconstruction of a house at Ur.

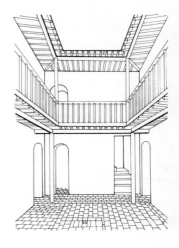

Top: reconstruction of the Ziggurat of Ur. A triple staircase led up to a sanctuary where king and priests performed sacred rites. The perfectly fired square burnt-bricks of the casing are the work of Ur-Nammu (about 2100 B.C.), whose name is stamped on them. *Bottom:* the Ziggurat photographed in 1955 during excavation. Two of the staircases can be seen.

The streets of Ur were narrow, winding and unpaved. Many were blocked with the open stalls of bazaars and markets.

Beyond the city walls were the cornfields and pastures where the farmers and labourers had their homes, and tilled the wide, fertile plain on which the great city depended.

Civilization

In the Old Stone Age man had been a primitive hunter, hard put to keep himself alive at all. In the New Stone Age the farmers still had to devote most of their time and energy to growing food.

But now, in Bronze Age Sumer, because of efficient farming, and because men had learned to combine together as never before, there was time and energy to spare. As a result, instead of everyone merely growing food, craftsmen were able to specialize, and thereby improve their work; merchants could travel to far-off lands; great cities could be built; kings could erect fine palaces; and priests serve their gods in awe-inspiring temples. As a result too, writing was invented, a calendar devised, while mathematics and astronomy, literature and music began to develop.

All these things mean that the Sumerians had created the earliest known civilization.

War

But there was one aspect of life in Sumer that was not so attractive. On the 'Royal Standard' of Ur, one side shows peaceful scenes. The other side depicts the army of the city, with its war chariots and helmeted shock troops. Already, alongside the useful and creative arts of peace, the Sumerians were developing the wasteful and destructive arts of war. Already, some men were specializing in killing their fellows.

Unfortunately, it was necessary for Ur to have this army. The increasing wealth of the Sumerian cities was attracting the marauding tribes of the highlands on the one side of Mesopotamia, and of the desert on the other.

Details of the 'Royal Standard' of Ur, an oblong box about 18 inches long, found in the Royal Tombs. *Above:* peace side. Men bring cattle and other gifts to the court of the king, who is banqueting to the sound of music.

Below: war side. There is a cavalry fight, an infantry battle and prisoners taken.

Yet the Sumerians did not only use such forces to defend themselves from raiding foreign tribes. Each city had its own king and was originally independent. But the cities were constantly quarrelling among themselves. Ur eventually succeeded in gaining control over Sumer. Later, however, she was overthrown by Lagash. After this, the leadership shifted from city to city, while the land itself was steadily weakened.

In the end, Sumer was conquered by one of the raiding peoples she had always feared.

Dates to remember

before 4000 B.C.   Men settle in Sumer
about 3500 B.C.   The earliest cities arise in Sumer
about 3500 B.C.   The beginning of writing and bronze-working

Things to discuss

Would you have preferred to live in the Old Stone Age, the New Stone Age, or the Bronze Age?

Things to do

1   By using other books, find out all you can about the Royal Tombs at Ur. Draw a plan of one of the tombs. Say why you think the king's bodyguard, musicians and servants were put to death for burial with him.
2   Using ink and a wedge-shaped piece of potato, stamp out the Sumerian signs shown in columns 3 and 4 on page 47. Notice how much easier it is to make the signs in column 4 than those in column 3. Why is this?
3   Try writing a few names or words, using the Sumerian picture-for-sound method. Here are two words to begin with: Gateshead, Churchill.
4   Turn back to page 48 and reread the description of the Sumerian schoolboy's day. Make a list of the offences he committed. Which of these would be offences in your school? How many times was the boy whipped? Why do you think his writing exercise may have been less satisfactory than usual?

Books to read

R. Carrington, *Ancient Sumer*, Chatto & Windus
R. Fawcett, *Sumer*, Gawthorn
H. W. F. Saggs, *Everyday Life in Babylonia and Assyria*, Batsford

Chapter 4
The first nation: Egypt

The land of Egypt

Modern Egypt is a large square-shaped country in the north-east corner of the continent of Africa. It covers an area of 386,000 square miles. Yet of this, all but 14,000 square miles is barren desert. The only part which is not desert is the Nile valley. Here the soil is as rich and fertile as any found on earth.

Ancient Egypt consisted simply of the Nile Valley. Between modern Aswan in the south and modern Cairo in the north this is a narrow corridor, varying in width from ten to fifteen miles, and shut in by steep cliffs on either side. North of Cairo, where the cliffs end, the Nile divides into many channels, forming a flat, low-lying delta.

Because hardly any rain falls in Egypt, the Nile valley, too, would be desert if it were not for the summer rains on the Abyssinian mountains. These cause the river to flood every year, so that from mid-August to October, most of the valley is under water. When the flood subsides, it leaves behind a thin layer of black mud, or silt, which is very fertile.

But originally the floods did not subside. About 5000 B.C., when the first settlers arrived from the surrounding deserts, they found that most of the valley was covered by permanent swamps. These formed a dense jungle of papyrus reeds which sheltered not only waterfowl and game, but also dangerous crocodiles and hippopotami. Only here and there, on patches of higher ground, could the settlers plant and harvest their first crops.

Before more land could be cultivated, some form of irrigation system had to be made. It is true that this was a much easier task than in Sumer (see pages 37–8). The Euphrates was a treacherous river and had at all costs to be kept within its own bed. But the Nile could safely be allowed to flood out over the land every autumn. Nevertheless, canals were still required to drain off the water, so that crops could be sown; and later to supply it during the otherwise waterless spring and summer seasons.

In Egypt, as in Sumer, the need for an irrigation system led the farmers to join together and co-operate. Indeed, the banding together of men went much further. Sumer remained a land of

A drawing from the mace-head of the Scorpion king shows him excavating a canal amidst a scene of rejoicing. The importance of irrigation is clearly suggested by this symbolic act. The king is wearing the white crown of Upper Egypt and reigned shortly before Narmer united Upper and Lower Egypt.

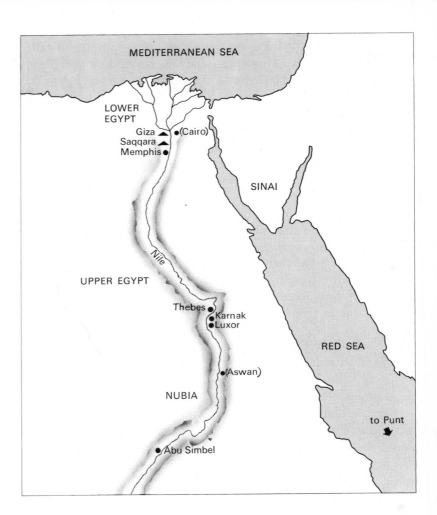

MEDITERRANEAN SEA

LOWER
EGYPT

Giza
Saqqara
Memphis ●

● (Cairo)

SINAI

Nile

UPPER EGYPT

Thebes ●
● Karnak
● Luxor

RED SEA

● (Aswan)

NUBIA

to Punt

● Abu Simbel

Chief cities of Upper (South)
and Lower (North) Egypt.

small city-states. The people of Egypt became united under the rule of a single king, making Egypt the first nation in history.

The union of Egypt

The earliest settlers lived in small villages. Because of the narrowness of the valley, the villages were packed closely together, and there were often quarrels between them, about such things as water rights, and which village should farm a particular piece of land. Eventually, the leader of one village in a particular district gained control over many neighbouring villages. From then onwards, this local chieftain settled all disputes. He also controlled the irrigation trenches and canals, defended the area, and acted as chief priest to the local god.

59

Later still, the districts or nomes as they came to be called were welded into two kingdoms. One was based on Upper Egypt (i.e. between Cairo and Aswan); the other on Lower Egypt (i.e. the delta). The king of Upper or South Egypt wore a white crown which was shaped like illustration 1. The king of Lower or North Egypt wore a red crown which was shaped like illustration 2. Finally, about 3100 B.C., a powerful king of South Egypt conquered the Northern kingdom and so became the first pharaoh of all Egypt. His legendary name was Menes, and his real name was probably King Narmer.

The famous Narmer palette commemorates this victory of the South, and the union of the whole land. On one side of the palette, Narmer wears the white crown of his own land. He is striking down a Northern enemy held by the hair. The other side shows the king wearing the red crown of North Egypt, the land he has just conquered. Behind him is his sandal-bearer and foot-washer, and in front of him four standard-bearers and a priest. The king is going towards two rows of corpses, which have had their heads cut off and placed between their legs. These are some of the unfortunate Northerners. Below this scene are two fabulous monsters with their long necks intertwined, perhaps to symbolize the union of the two kingdoms.

Narmer himself sometimes used the red crown and sometimes the white. But later the two crowns were combined, see illustration 3 above.

Thereafter, this double crown was always worn by the pharaoh who, even in later times, was addressed by the title: 'the Lord of the Two Lands'.

What the pharaoh's government did for Egypt

The pharaoh's government did many important things. It protected the land and its inhabitants by organizing a system of frontier defences to keep out the raiding war-bands which sometimes attacked from the desert.

The preserving of internal peace was another of the pharaoh's tasks. The people of a nation can only live together without quarrelling if there are good laws, and if the rulers make sure that the laws are obeyed. Many of the laws of the Egyptians were traditional: that is to say, they had grown up gradually, over the centuries. But the pharaoh could make new laws, and did so, whenever he thought it was necessary. Any order of the pharaoh automatically became law.

When an Egyptian broke one of the laws, or had a dispute with

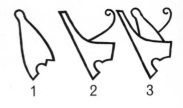

1 White crown of Upper (South) Egypt.
2 Red crown of Lower (North) Egypt.
3 Double crown.

Narmer striking down a Northern enemy (from the Narmer palette).

Narmer palette. At the top
(*centre*) is a palace building
and on either side the head of
the Egyptian mother goddess,
Hathor. She is shown with a
human face but with the ears
and horns of a cow. At the
bottom of the palette the king
is represented as a strong bull
breaking down the walls of an
enemy township. The two
animals with long necks are
probably mythical.

his neighbour, the case would be tried in his local court where the pharaoh's ministers or officials acted as judges. A man who lost his case in the local court had the right to appeal to the Great Court, and even to the pharaoh himself.

Another thing the pharaoh's government did was to look after the irrigation system. When Egypt became united, all the local systems of canals were brought together into one enormous national system, and this was controlled from the capital. The peasants were called up in labour gangs, both to keep existing canals clean and in good repair, and to dig new canals. In this way higher land, which was beyond the reach of the flood, was brought under cultivation, and more food could be grown. Royal officials kept careful records of the behaviour of the river, so that they could give due warning of the flood. When the flood came they measured its height. If the water-level was below a certain point, they knew that there would be famine in the land.

But the pharaoh's government took precautions against this misfortune also. Surplus corn stored in the royal granaries during good seasons provided the extra food that was needed when the harvest failed. The Old Testament story of Joseph tells of a failure of the harvest.

Wooden figure of a high Egyptian official, dated about 1400 B.C. He is bare-footed and wears a tight-fitting pleated linen garment with a wide skirt. This and the other wooden models illustrating this chapter were found in Egyptian tombs; most of them can be seen today in the British Museum.

Left: wooden model of a granary. Against the back wall, a foreman *(right)* superintends the work of storing grain, while a scribe enters details of the corn received on a board.

Ancient Egypt was not a particularly large country, only about a quarter the size of England. But it was extremely long and narrow, and therefore not easy to govern from one centre. Narmer built his capital at Memphis, at the apex of the delta (near modern Cairo). It was thus on the border, between the Upper and Lower kingdoms.

The king had two kinds of officials. First, there were the central officials who lived and worked in the capital. The most important of these was the vizier, who was the pharaoh's chief minister. Second, the pharaoh had local officials scattered throughout the land. The system of local government was based on the old nomes. But in place of a tribal chieftain each of these forty-two districts now had a governor who carried out the king's orders.

One of the main tasks of central and local officials was the collection of taxes. These were not paid in coined money, since coinage had not yet been invented. Instead people paid in kind. Collecting the taxes, therefore, was an awkward and complicated business. The livestock and grain had to be stored in the royal granaries, cattleyards and warehouses. Here thousands of clerks kept careful records of the king's accounts. They had lists of the taxpayers' names, and knew exactly how much each person owed. When the tax was paid they issued receipts, in much the same way as receipts are issued today.

The pharaoh's government did many other things which we have not time to discuss in detail. It gave the country a calendar, and a standardized system of weights and measures. Foreign trade depended almost entirely on the pharaoh. Royal expeditions

Measuring land in ancient Egypt using lengths of cord. The two fully clothed figures are scribes. Each carries his scribe's palette, a rectangular block of wood holding ink and brushes. The corn in the field looks ready for harvesting. This is part of an Egyptian wall painting.

brought wood from Syria, lead and silver from Asia and copper from Sinai. The government also sent expeditions down the Red Sea to the land of Punt (now Somaliland), where ebony, ivory and fragrant gums could be obtained.

The pharaoh did much to encourage initiative and experiment. He employed large numbers of skilled craftsmen, which meant that the various arts and techniques of civilization developed rapidly. Similarly he encouraged learning.

Really capable people could find almost limitless opportunities to use their knowledge and skill in the pharaoh's service. That is why in the Egypt of this time we meet the first great men of history – or at least the first men who were great and famous because of their own abilities and not because they were kings.

Imhotep

One such man was Imhotep, who lived in the 27th century B.C. He was King Zoser's vizier, and built as a tomb for his pharaoh the famous Step Pyramid at Saqqara. This was the wonder of its age. In addition to being the first pyramid, it was one of the first large stone buildings the world had ever seen. Around the pyramid he erected several other tombs and tomb chapels (see opposite). All

The Step Pyramid. The six rectangular terraces rise to a height of about 200 feet. From its state of preservation it is difficult to believe that it has stood for over 4,500 years.

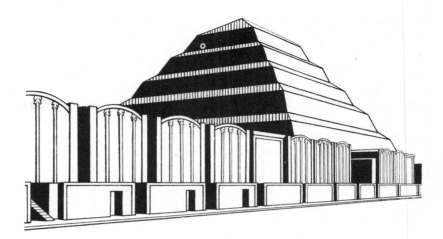

Reconstruction of the tomb chapels beside the Step Pyramid.

Imhotep. This silver statuette shows him holding a roll of papyrus on his knees, perhaps a learned medical text. All 'books' were in the form of rolls in ancient Egypt. (The statuette is a late one, dated 660 B.C.)

these buildings were so marvellously planned and designed that Imhotep is still acknowledged as one of the world's greatest architects. Yet even that was not enough for this astonishingly able and energetic man. Somehow he found time to study astronomy, medicine, and many other subjects. His medical knowledge impressed Egyptians and centuries after his death they began worshipping him as the god of medicine. Imhotep obviously did enough work to last several lifetimes, rather than one. Yet such a man only had the opportunity to accomplish all this because he had been raised up in the pharaoh's service.

The pharaoh

In countless ways then, the Egyptians derived great benefits from their system of national government. However, this was only one reason they stayed a united people throughout ancient times. Another reason was their national pride and strong sense of belonging together. Egyptians felt that they were privileged to have been born in Egypt, which they regarded as infinitely superior to other countries. All other lands, they thought, were cold and dark, and the people who lived in them more akin to animals than to human beings. But perhaps it was the ancient Egyptian's feelings and beliefs about the pharaoh that provided the strongest unifying force of all.

In Sumer, the king of each city was thought to be the chief servant of the city's god. The Egyptian idea of kingship went further than this. They thought that their king was himself a living god, a divine ruler who had magic control over the weather, and the Nile; and who alone brought safety, prosperity and happiness to the nation.

Because of these ideas, the pharaoh was the richest and most powerful ruler the world had ever known. Almost a fifth of the nation's wealth flowed into his treasury in taxes. Yet no Egyptian begrudged him this. For they believed that the whole land belonged to him, as well as all its people. So reverenced was the divine king that his subjects dared not mention him by name. They only spoke of the palace in which he lived. That is why they called him pharaoh, which means 'great house'.

When we realize how much the pharaoh meant to the Egyptians, it is easier to understand how the pyramids came to be built. Since he was a god, he could not possibly be allowed to die. Yet his spirit – so it was believed – would survive only if his body were preserved, together with everything that was needed for its future well-being. The pyramids, therefore were designed as soul-houses that would last for ever, as eternal dwelling places for the god-kings. So, protected and cared for, the dead pharaohs would be able to continue their magic work for the 'beloved land'.

From Giza, a little west of modern Cairo (and close to the ancient royal capital of Memphis) an astonishing line of pyramids stretches southwards for sixty miles. Here, one after another, for about 500 years (from the 27th to the 22nd centuries B.C.) the pharaohs of Egypt were entombed. Thirty pyramids still stand, and there are the remains of thirty more.

We have already spoken of the Step Pyramid, built by Imhotep. This was small, however, when compared with the Great Pyramid built for Cheops (or Khufu). This pyramid measures 755 feet on each side, covers 13 acres and rises to a height of 481 feet; over 100 feet higher than St Paul's Cathedral. It is a solid mountain of uncemented masonry, containing 2,300,000 blocks of stone which average $2\frac{1}{2}$ tons each. Tradition says that 100,000 men worked on it for twenty years.

This can well be imagined, for the amount of labour involved must have been tremendous. First the site had to be cleared of sand and the rock levelled. Next a subterranean passageway and chamber were hollowed out. Meanwhile, stone for the pyramid itself was quarried. That used for the core could be found near at hand, but the fine limestone for the outer facing came from the desert, between the Nile and the Red Sea. Using copper tools, skilled masons would cut and dress these stones at the quarry so that they fitted each other perfectly. Then, when the flood came, thousands of labourers, who could not work on the land during this season, dragged the huge blocks, on rollers and wooden sledges, to the edge of the water. Here they were loaded on to barges, and ferried across

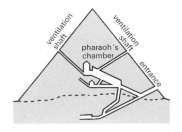

Above: section of the Great Pyramid of Cheops. At first a subterranean chamber was excavated at the end of a long descending passageway. Perhaps this was originally intended to take the pharaoh's body, but for some reason it was abandoned and two chambers constructed in the pyramid itself. The upper one, known as the pharaoh's chamber, is thought to be the one in which Cheops was buried.

Opposite page

Above: sphinx and the Great Pyramid. The sphinx is a human-headed lion, 187 feet long and 66 feet high.

Below: buildings associated with a pyramid. The mastaba was the tomb of a nobleman. Once the funeral boats had brought the pharaoh's body to the pyramid, it was sealed up 'for ever'.

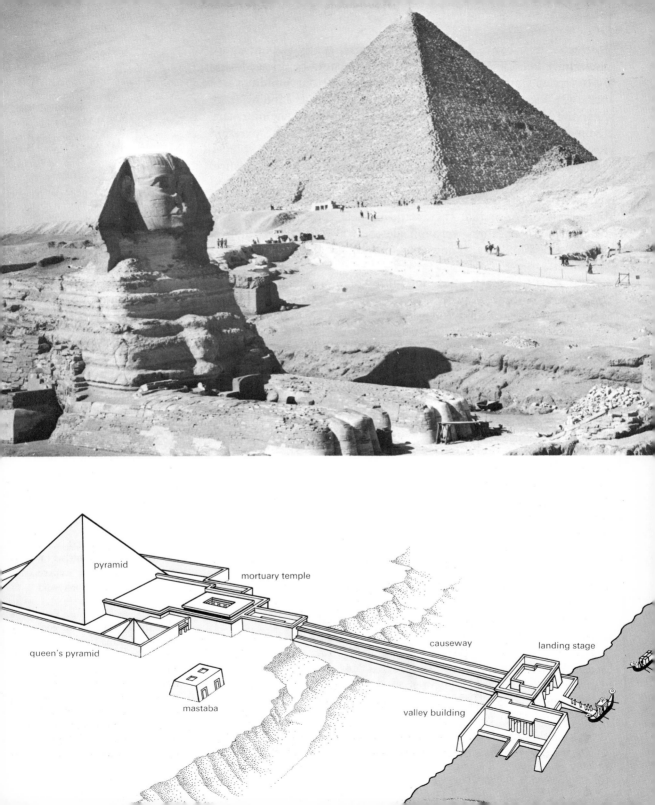

pyramid

mortuary temple

queen's pyramid

causeway

landing stage

mastaba

valley building

to the western bank. As the pyramid grew, gently sloping ramps must have been used, up which the stones could be dragged.

A typical pyramid consisted of a group of four buildings (see page 63). First there was a valley building, with its landing-stage near the Nile. From this a covered causeway led to the mortuary temple dedicated to the dead pharaoh; then came the pyramid itself, surrounded by a high wall.

Around the pharaoh's tomb, and inside the walled enclosure, were smaller pyramids made to receive the pharaoh's wives and daughters when they died. The great nobles of the court were also buried close by, so that they could be near their master even in death. But their tombs were outside the walls, and were smaller, flat-topped buildings, known as mastabas. Only royalty had pyramids.

The Egyptians, like the Sumerians, worshipped countless gods. But many of these were local deities, and need not concern us. Throughout the land, however, two gods were universally worshipped. One was the sun (called at different times, and in different connexions, Horus, Re, Amun-Re or Aton). The other great god was Osiris, god of the Nile and of the afterworld.

The living pharaoh was supposed to be the living Horus, or the son of Re. In other words, he had his power from the sun. On death, though, he was believed to become one with Osiris. At first the pharaoh alone had this privilege. But later the nobles began to believe that they would join Osiris at death, and eventually, even the common people. However, by this time it was also thought that Osiris would judge the dead according to their earthly conduct. Only the good would be admitted to an afterlife. This idea of a

Above: Osiris. Since he was believed to be both the dead king and the king of the dead, he is depicted as a man swathed in mummy wrappings. He wears on his head a royal crown decorated with ostrich feathers. In his hands he holds emblems of supreme power: the sceptre, in the form of a crook, and the whip.

Left: the Egyptian Sun god, Re. His head is that of a falcon. Above it is a sun-disc with a terrible sacred snake coiled round it: this destroyed the god's enemies by spitting flames. The boat in which Re is seated was thought to carry him on his daily journeys across the heavens.

Musicians, from a tomb-painting. One (second from the right) is playing a double-flute; another (centre) the lute; a third (left) a lute-like instrument.

Below: wooden model of a boat with rowers, from a tomb. The large oar (left) is the steering oar – compare with Re's boat opposite. Such boats were not sea-going vessels but were used for traffic backwards and forwards along the Nile.

judgement of the dead, first met in Egypt, is one that becomes very important later, in Christianity.

The Egyptians were convinced that a man's spirit could not survive without his body. To preserve the bodies of the pharaohs, and later of the nobles, they treated the corpse with natron and other substances, and then wrapped it in linen bandages. Many of these mummies, as they are called, have survived down to the present day. The Egyptians did not rely only on mummification: in case the body decayed they made statues of the dead man, believing that, in the last resort, his spirit would be able to use one of these as a substitute body.

Since they thought that the next life was much the same as this one, a great man had his personal possessions and furniture buried with him, as well as a plentiful supply of food. Some things, though, could not be buried. So they made models like the granary on page 58, and the boat below; or they painted pictures on the walls

of tombs, like the musicians on page 65, or the nobleman's garden and the duck-hunting scene on page 71.

The effort and resources needed to build pyramids was so great that from the 25th century B.C. they had perforce to become smaller and smaller, the later pharaohs being buried, not in pyramids, but in rock tombs. Yet the grave equipment remained as extravagant as before. When Howard Carter discovered the tomb of Tutankhamen in 1922 it proved to contain 'the most incredible burial treasure ever found'. Everything was still perfectly preserved in the burial chamber where it had lain for over 3,000 years – since 1300 B.C. There was beautiful jewellery and furniture which the king had used in life, including his gold-plated throne. Other articles had been specially made for the burial: three funeral beds, the gold-plated shrine, and a funeral mask of solid gold.

Tutankhamen's tomb was that of a mere boy pharaoh, and leads us to wonder how fabulous some of the great pharaohs' tombs – long since plundered by tomb robbers – must once have been.

With all this treasure going into the ground, the cost of caring for the dead must have been a tremendous burden on the living. Moreover, we cannot help reflecting that the majority of Egyptians

Right: Tutankhamen's tomb: the entrance to the room called by Howard Carter 'the Treasury'. In the centre is a great chest of gilded wood with its carrying poles. On the top sits Anubis, a god of the dead and the protector of burials, who was always represented as a black jackal or dog. Notice the linen cloth wrapped round him.

Below: Tutankhamen's throne, covered in heavy sheet gold. *Below left:* details of its back. Tutankhamen's queen appears to be putting the finishing touches to the king's toilet by anointing his collarette. Against a background of gold, the garments worn by the royal couple are of silver, and their flesh is of reddish glass.

could ill afford it. They were poverty-stricken peasants who could have lived much more comfortable lives if they had not had to pay the high taxes needed for royal burials. But this is to look at the matter through modern eyes. Such ideas probably never occurred to ancient Egyptians: they were too convinced of the importance of the pharaoh. 'What is the King of Upper and Lower Egypt?' wrote a vizier in about 1500 B.C. 'He is a god by whose dealings one lives, the father and mother of all men, alone by himself, without an equal.'

Art and architecture

The building and equipping of the tombs was a great human achievement. The pyramids prove that the Egyptians were superb architects. They built them to last for ever, and it looks as though many of them will. Moreover, their buildings were wonderfully designed and decorated, as well as being long-lasting. We see this particularly in the temples, where stone columns similar to those supporting many of our own buildings were first used.

Another clever invention was the clerestory (or clear-story) illustrated right. Again, this idea was handed down through the ages until eventually it was used, as a means of admitting more light, in Christian churches.

In equipping the tombs and temples, sculptors had almost as much to do as the architects, and their work too was remarkable. They carved magnificent portrait statues of the dead pharaohs and nobles. The carvings were in wood or stone and were often painted

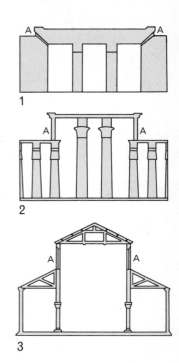

Development of the clerestory.
1 The earliest clerestory at Giza (about 2500 B.C.). This great hall would have been very dark but for the light chutes (AA).
2 Hall at Karnak, built over 1,000 years later. The narrow chutes have become stately clerestory windows.
3 Christian basilica church of 4th century A.D., showing how the clerestory was used by the Romans. Many medieval churches have a similar clerestory.

Left: stone columns at the temple of Luxor, built about 1400 B.C. Notice how huge and elaborate they are compared with Imhotep's columns of over a thousand years earlier (see page 61).

Above: wall relief of about 2360 B.C. showing harvesting. *Top row:* asses are being assembled and fitted with panniers (baskets) for carrying corn. *Bottom row:* reapers are cutting corn, while a man plays on the flute to keep them working in time.

Below: another carving in low relief of about 2600 B.C.

in colours chosen to make the statue as lifelike as possible.

Perhaps the most famous Egyptian statue is the sphinx which stands in the cemetery at Giza (see page 63). The head is probably a portrait of Chephren, son of Cheops, the pharaoh buried in the Great Pyramid, but the body is that of a lion, to symbolize royalty. This statue, which is the largest portrait ever made, is hewn from an upstanding piece of rock, so it still remains attached to the ground.

Sculptors also carved wall pictures in the tombs. The illustration above shows one of these carvings in low relief. It depicts harvesting scenes on the dead man's estate, and the original is brightly coloured. At first you may think it is rather badly drawn. For instance, the artist cared nothing for the laws of perspective, so that things in the distance are shown just as large as things that are close to (see the asses in the top row). The posture of the human figures in the picture is also rather odd. The head and legs are seen from the side, in profile; but the body is drawn as if from the front. If you try to stand in this position yourself, you will realize how unnatural it is. However, this does not mean that the Egyptians were bad artists. This was their traditional way of drawing. Many modern artists, like Picasso, admire the art of the ancient Egyptians, simply because they did not slavishly copy nature. They admire it also for its freshness and vitality.

Some of the finest work of the Egyptian craftsmen also found its way into the tombs. Egyptian pottery and jewellery and metalwork were as fine as that made in Sumer. One industry which was unknown in Sumer was practised here. This was the making of delicate glass vessels.

Life on a nobleman's estate

The sculptures and paintings, and the things buried in tombs, help us to form a good idea of how the nobles and other rich Egyptians lived.

A rich man's house was large and stood in its own grounds, often surrounded by a high wall. It was built of wood and sun-baked brick, and contained many spacious rooms, with gaily painted walls and ceilings. At the centre of the house was the biggest room of all, that in which the master entertained his guests. Leading off from this were several private chambers, and a bedroom for each member of the family. The house had an indoor toilet and a bathroom. A staircase led up to the flat roof, which, with its large coloured awning, was frequently used as an open-air sitting-room.

If it were possible for you to visit such a house, one of the things which would particularly surprise you would be the way it was furnished. Five thousand years ago, rich people in Egypt had furniture which is not so very different from that of our own day. They had wooden-framed beds similar to ours, though instead of a pillow they used a wooden headrest. Their chairs and stools were quite modern in appearance. But they had no large tables; only small ones, at which they ate their meals.

A nobleman lived a happy and comfortable life. Part of the day he spent looking after business affairs. But there was plenty of leisure too. When he felt like it, he could go duck hunting in the marshes, taking his wife and children with him to punt the skiff through the reeds. Then there was the lovely garden which surrounded his house. Here, sitting in the shade of the trees, he would challenge his wife to a game of draughts, or listen to a group of musicians playing on the harp, pipe and lute. Meanwhile, his children amused themselves with the pet monkey, swam in the garden pool, or perhaps played at one of the many ball games.

Wooden model of a girl playing a harp dated about 1200 B.C.

Below: Egyptian furniture
1 Stool with legs carved and decorated to represent the neck and head of ducks.
2 Folding bed from Tutankhamen's tomb.
3 Chair, with a high back.

1   2   3

Right: nobleman's garden, with a fishpond and a variety of fruit trees. The painting shows Egyptian disregard for perspective. Trees, fish and birds are side view; the pond is shown as a plan.

Duck hunting in the marshes. The nobleman stands in his skiff, accompanied by two women, perhaps his wife and daughter. He holds a throwing-stick (shaped like a snake) in his left hand. Cats were used to flush the birds and one can be seen leaping into the air just in front of him. There are papyrus reeds on the left.

Life of the peasant

Only a very few Egyptians were able to live in this pleasant and leisurely way. By contrast, the life of the peasant, on whose toil the wealth of Egypt depended, was without luxuries of any kind. Many of the peasants were serfs or slaves belonging to the pharaoh or one of the nobles. When a noble sold an estate he sold the serfs with it; so in this respect they counted for little more than cattle.

The serfs' life was hard. They toiled on the land from dawn to sunset, though there was always a rest in the middle of the day when it was too hot for work. They ploughed and sowed and watered the fields; and when the time came they gathered in the harvest.

In the flood season, nothing much could be done on the farms. Yet even then there was no rest for the peasants. They found themselves conscripted into one of the pharaoh's labour gangs: digging a new canal, quarrying and transporting stone, or helping to erect the latest pyramid.

A peasant's house was built of sun-baked brick, and generally had four rooms: an entrance hall, a living-room, one bedroom and a kitchen. As in the rich man's house, a stairway led up to the roof, which was used for all sorts of purposes. There was little furniture: a bed or two, stools, and clay vessels for storage and cooking.

We have spoken of the life of the great nobleman and of the humble peasant. Between these extremes were the lesser government officials, the scribes, craftsmen and traders. In early Egypt such people were employed either by the pharaoh or on the estates of rich landowners. As a rule, they enjoyed a higher standard of life than the peasants; nevertheless, they remained servants, with no chance of setting up in business on their own.

Above: model of what a peasant's house probably looked like. Pottery models of such houses were often found in the graves of poorer people.

Model of a bakery and brewery of about 2000 B.C. The men standing at the back are grinding corn while those squatting are sifting flour. The square blocks at the front are ovens for baking bread, the round ones vats for brewing beer.

In this respect early Egypt differed from Sumer, where merchants and craftsmen worked for themselves, and so formed a middle class of fairly independent people. From about 2000 B.C., however, a middle class of this kind began to grow in Egypt also.

But whether we are thinking of 3000 B.C. or 2000 B.C., of Sumer or Egypt, of servile peasants or of independent craftsmen, one important point has to be remembered. Although we have seen the arrival of the first cities and the first city-dwellers, we cannot yet speak of *citizens*.

A citizen is a person who has the right to take some part in the government of his city or country. But in the early civilizations, the common people had no say whatever in such matters. In Sumer kings and priests ruled; in Egypt government was in the hands of the pharaoh, a living god. Another mark of citizenship is personal freedom: the right of each individual to live his life as he chooses. In Sumer and Egypt very few enjoyed even this right.

The time would come when a later civilization would discover a form of government in which ordinary people would have more say, both in their own destiny, and in the destiny of their city or nation. But this was not to happen for another 2,000 years.

Above: a peasant hoeing.

Below: a peasant ploughing. Notice how the two oxen are yoked to the plough.

Writing and learning

With the two earliest civilizations, we have passed from prehistory to history, for both these people have left records in writing.

But writing had not yet spread to other lands. It did not reach Britain until the Romans brought it, under 2,000 years ago. For a long time, Britain, like most other parts of the world, was to remain in 'prehistoric times'.

The Egyptians probably learned the art of writing from the Sumerians. Like them, they soon decided that, instead of their signs standing for things and ideas, they would make some of them stand for sounds.

Later on, they went a stage further. All the Sumerian sound-signs represented *syllables*, but the Egyptians invented about twenty-four signs which stood for *simple sounds*.

They were thus the first people to use proper alphabetic signs, or real letters; though, as you will see by studying the table, they had letters for consonants only, but none for vowels. Unfortunately, too, alongside the new alphabetic signs, they continued to use many hundreds of old ones. So they failed to invent true alphabetic writing, which depends on the use of alphabetical signs *alone*.

Egyptian schools were run on similar lines to Sumerian ones. As in Sumer, too, only the fortunate few had the chance to attend. Probably many children would have resented the hard work involved in any case. Yet, a sound education was essential to anyone who wished to make a good career for himself, as a priest, a government official, or a scribe, for example. It is not unusual for parents to be more aware of this fact than their children. Here is an Egyptian father, taking his son to school, and lecturing to him on the way, about the tremendous difference education will make to his future career:

I have never seen the smith as an ambassador, but I have seen the smith at his work at the mouth of his furnace, his fingers like the crocodile's, and he stank more than fishes' eggs . . . . The stonemason finds his work in every kind of hard stone. When he has finished his labours his arms are worn out, and he sleeps all doubled up until sunrise. His knees and his spine are broken . . . . The barber shaves from morning to night . . . . He wears out his arms to fill his stomach, like bees eating their honey . . . . The farmer wears the same clothes for all times. His voice is as raucous as a crow's. His fingers are always busy, his arms are dried up by the wind. He takes his rest – when he does get any rest – in the mud. If he's in good health he shares good health with the beasts; if he is ill his bed is the bare earth in the middle

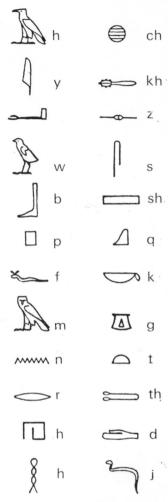

The twenty-four sound signs. The third sign in the left-hand column is a guttural sound, produced at the back of the throat and not in use in English.

of his beasts. Scarcely does he get home at night when off he has to start again. Apply your heart to learning. In truth there is nothing that can compare with it. If you have profited by a single day at school it is a gain for eternity.

One respect in which Egyptian schools did differ from Sumerian ones is that the boys practised their writing with more convenient materials. The Egyptians did not follow the Sumerian custom of writing on clay. Throughout their history they continued carving important texts on stone. But, realizing that this was useless for everyday purposes, they soon invented pen, ink and paper.

A pointed reed cut from the marshes served as a pen. For ink they mixed soot with water, adding a little vegetable gum. They made their paper by splitting papyrus reeds into thin strips and pasting them together, so that each strip overlapped the next. Our word 'paper', which is 'papyrus' slightly altered, stands as a permanent reminder that we owe this way of writing to the ancient Egyptians.

Egyptian men of learning were soon using these new materials to set down their ideas on subjects like arithmetic, astronomy and medicine. And there were works of religion, poetry and legend, too.

In less kind climates the paper on which they were written would have rotted away long ago. But in Egypt this frail material has been miraculously preserved in the warm dry conditions. So, with their literature and art, and the things they left buried in the tombs, we know more about the ancient Egyptians than we can possibly know about any earlier people – or about many later ones.

The Rhind Papyrus of about 1500 B.C. This is a 'book' of mathematical problems with their solutions. The section deals with the measurement of the slope of a pyramid. Note the texture of the papyrus.

Dates to remember

about 3100 B.C.   The union of Egypt
27th century B.C.   Imhotep lived
from 27th to 22nd century B.C. Age of the pyramids
                                 (Old Kingdom)

Things to do

1 Imagine that you have been able to spend a day in ancient Egypt. During it, you visited a nobleman's house, and the house of a peasant. Write something about each type of house, and also about the life of the nobleman and the peasant. Use other books to help you, as well as this one; and, if possible, visit a museum where Egyptian things may be seen.

2 Study the illustrations in this chapter, and any other examples of Egyptian art you can find. Then make a drawing showing life in your own school, doing it entirely in the Egyptian style.

3 How did the Egyptians get the huge blocks of stone up to the top of the pyramids? No one knows in detail. Imagine you were the engineer in charge and explain, in words and drawings, *exactly* how you would plan this difficult operation. Incidentally, the Egyptians had no pulleys.

4 One of the most dramatic of all archaeological discoveries was the excavation of the tomb of Tutankhamen. Find out all you can about this. An excellent collection of photographs will be found in the book called *Tutankhamen,* by C. Desroches-Noblecourt.

5 Write a few words using the Egyptian alphabet . You will have to leave out the vowels. See if you can find out how the Egyptians got round the difficulty of having no vowels.

6 This chapter has concentrated mainly on Egypt during the age of the pyramids, or the Old Kingdom, though many of the illustrations come from a later period. From other books find out something about Egypt during the Middle and New Kingdoms. Make notes on the ways in which life changed. For instance, during the Old Kingdom, as described on page 61, the pharaoh was considered a sublime being, far beyond the reach of ordinary mortals; but in the Middle Kingdom he became more 'human', being thought of as the 'watchful shepherd' of his people.

Books to read

R. Carrington, *Ancient Egypt,* Chatto & Windus
R. Fawcett, *Egypt,* Gawthorn

Egyptian noblewomen were skilled in the use of cosmetics. *Above:* applying lipstick.

Right: wooden toilet chest which belonged to the wife of an Egyptian scribe, in about 1300 B.C.

H. E. L. Mellersh, *Finding out about Ancient Egypt*, Muller
E. J. Sheppard, *Ancient Egypt*, Longmans
B. Sewell and P. B. Lynch, *The Story of Ancient Egypt*, E. Arnold
H. and R. Leacroft, *The Buildings of Ancient Egypt*, Penguin

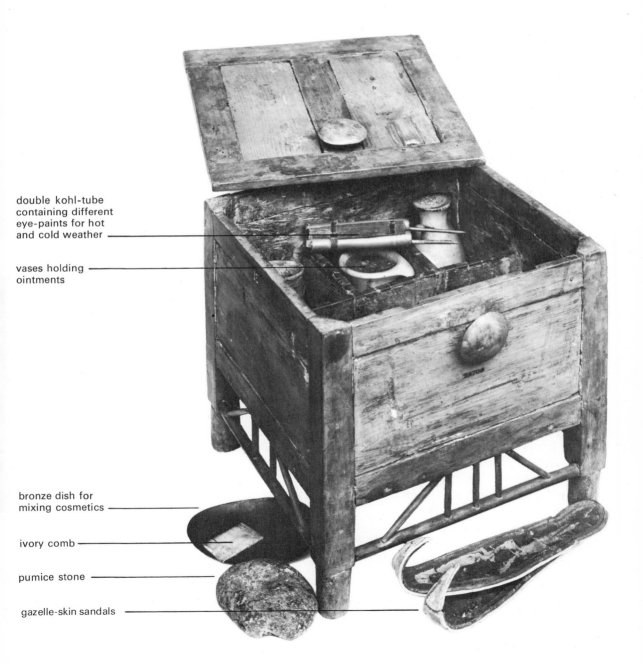

double kohl-tube containing different eye-paints for hot and cold weather

vases holding ointments

bronze dish for mixing cosmetics

ivory comb

pumice stone

gazelle-skin sandals

Chapter 5
The spread of civilization: India, China, Crete

Up to now, we have watched the rise of civilization in one part of the world, the Near East. As far as we know at present, this is where civilization first came into being. But it did not only develop here. Two very early civilizations also grew up in the Far East, in India and China.

Just as in Mesopotamia, so in the Far East, this development took place in the river valleys.

India

We saw in chapter 2 that the region over which the first farming villages are to be found included the Iranian Plateau. Immediately to the west of this was Mesopotamia, and the first people to settle in that land came from the Iranian Plateau. But, as the map below shows, to the east of the plateau, there is another great river valley, the Indus valley. In many ways this was

Early civilizations of the Old World.

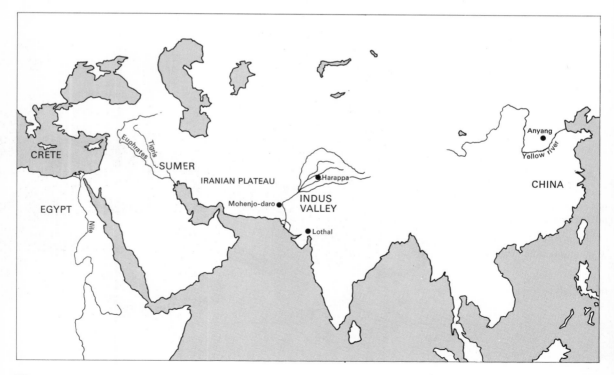

similar to the valleys of Mesopotamia. It is hardly surprising therefore, that the early farmers of the Iranian highlands – or at least their ideas – should have spread in this direction also. As a result, by about 2500 B.C., another civilization had been born.

Although it was not the first, this Indian civilization was one of the largest early civilizations. The area over which it spread forms a huge triangle with sides 950, 700 and 550 miles long. Yet we do not know the name of the great kingdom that was here, nor of the people who made it: we simply have to call it the 'Indus Valley' civilization.

Archaeologists have discovered the remains of about forty towns and villages which were once inhabited by the Indus Valley people. The best known of these are the two cities, Mohenjo-daro and Harappa, which were the largest and best organized cities of their time in India. Each was over three miles in circuit and had an area of almost one square mile. Since they were 350 miles apart, perhaps they were twin capitals of a northern and a southern kingdom, with the rivers Indus and Ravi linking them.

One of the astonishing things about Mohenjo-daro and Harappa is the amount of careful planning that had gone into them. Most

Excavating the remains of the citadel at Lothal, a small town of the Indus Valley civilization about 450 miles south-east of Mohenjo-daro. Beyond it stretches the hot, bare Indian plain.

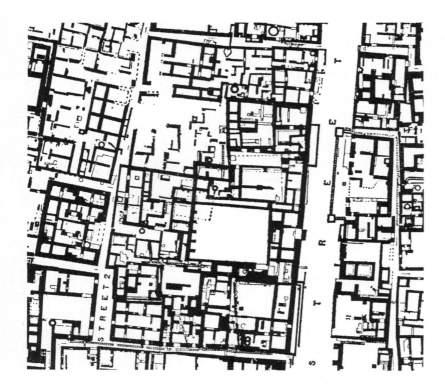

Left: plan of the residential area of Mohenjo-daro. As they have no gardens, the houses are tightly packed.

Well at Mohenjo-daro, which has remained intact for over 4,000 years.

of our towns in England were never planned at all; they were just allowed to grow haphazardly. Indeed, it is only in recent times that we have come to recognize the importance of town planning. The Indus Valley people realized it over 4,000 years ago, and were the first ever to do so.

Both towns were planned on exactly uniform lines. Both were built by the sides of a river. Both had a series of broad, straight streets running from north to south, while another series crossed them at right angles in an east–west direction. Thus each city was divided into a number of large, rectangular building blocks.

At Mohenjo-daro there were twelve of these blocks, in three rows of four. The central block on the western side was occupied by the citadel. This stood on a platform forty feet above the general level of the city. Surrounding and protecting it was a strong defensive wall with rectangular towers and monumental gateways.

It seems quite likely that these Indus Valley cities were ruled by a group of powerful priests, and that the citadels served as their headquarters. At Mohenjo-daro the buildings inside the wall included a pillared hall and a cloistered 'monastery' in

Above: Great Bath at Mohenjo-daro. Steps lead down to the floor of the bath. The brick piers beyond were part of the verandah which enclosed it on all sides.

which the priests may have lived. There was also the Great Bath (40 feet by 24 feet, with a depth of 8 feet) which was probably used for ritual bathing (still much practised in India).

Below the citadel to the east stretched the shops and houses of the town. Many of the houses obviously belonged to fairly wealthy people. They were built round a central courtyard like those of Sumer, and contained many rooms of various sizes, including a bathroom, with its brick-paved floor. A bath was taken, as in modern India, by pouring water over the body from a large jar. The water then ran away through a drain at one corner.

Mohenjo-daro is renowned for its strikingly efficient and 'modern' drainage system. Every house had its separate drain, which led into a main sewer running under the street. The sewers could be cleaned out by lifting man-hole covers, placed at regular intervals.

The Indus Valley people seem to have been particularly keen on cleanliness. Well-to-do householders had an ingenious way of getting rid of their refuse, by means of a rubbish chute which passed through the house wall and into a brick-built bin outside. So there was no need to go out to the dustbin!

Left: a main street of Mohenjo-daro. The main sewer is on the right with side drains running into it at regular intervals. In ancient times all drains were covered.

Clay model of a terrier-like dog with a collar, excavated at Mohenjo-daro.

Some of the better-class houses had only one floor, and some had two. A stairway led up to the roof which, as in other eastern lands, was much used by the family for all sorts of purposes.

Naturally, not all the townsfolk enjoyed such excellent accommodation. In the workmen's quarter of the city, the people lived in small, dingy, two-roomed cottages, built in monotonous rows. Nevertheless, in general, Mohenjo-daro and Harappa were the most impressive cities that had so far been built.

As in Mesopotamia and Egypt, the making of such cities was only possible because the Indus Valley people were highly successful farmers. The peasants who lived in the countryside must have been able to grow enough food to support the town populations as well as themselves.

Farming seems to have been controlled and organized from the cities. Today much of the Indus Valley is barren; but in ancient times, with its elaborate arrangement of banks, reservoirs and canals, it was amazingly fertile.

Each town had a large granary for the storage of corn, as well as municipal flour mills. Doubtless this corn was regularly collected from the countryside, in the form of taxes. Wheat, barley and peas were grown. So was the cotton plant which

Model of a two-wheeled
ox-cart excavated at Harappa.

Seals from Mohenjo-daro.
They depict an elephant
(below left) and a humped bull
(below right). Perhaps the
writing at the top gives the
owner's name; however, no
one has deciphered the Indus
Valley script.

provided India's main textile. In addition to the domestic animals found in the Near East, humped bulls and buffaloes were kept.

Industries thrived in the Indus Valley, too, particularly metalwork, pottery and brick-making. Then there was trading with Sumer and other lands. Among important Indian exports were cotton, pepper and spices.

For transport the Indians used camels and packhorses, while goats took goods over the mountains. Heavy loads were carried on two-wheeled ox-carts which are of exactly the same type as that found in India today. Even the width between the wheels has not changed. The wheel ruts discovered during the excavations at Harappa are 3 feet 6 inches apart, and that remains the gauge of the present-day Indian ox-cart. For water-transport there were boats with a high prow and stern, a central sail-mast, and a long steering oar.

In some ways Indian civilization does not seem to have been so advanced as those of Sumer and Egypt. Although they had a system of writing, no written records of the Indus Valley people have survived. The little writing that has come down to us is found on the seals which they used for stamping merchandise and other property.

Left: a bearded mån from Mohenjo-daro. His shawl is decorated with trefoils and, since this was a religious symbol, some people think he was a priest-king, or perhaps even a god.

Bronze dancing girl from Mohenjo-daro.

Compared with Egypt and Sumer, few art treasures have been excavated. Some of their pottery was rather fine; but apart from this, and the seals, the only other exciting things are works of sculpture. Among the best known pieces is the head of a bearded man which was discovered at Mohenjo-daro.

But if their art was not particularly remarkable, they undoubtedly had a highly developed religion. In fact, some of the beliefs and customs of Hinduism, which is still the chief religion of India, seem to have descended from this people. As we have seen, among the customs that may have been handed down was ritual bathing. One of the principal Hindu gods is called Siva (see page 193), and it is interesting to note that a little statue which closely resembles later effigies of Siva has been dug up at Mohenjo-daro, suggesting that he was already being worshipped by the Indus Valley people over 4,000 years ago.

China

The cradle of Chinese civilization was in the north of that vast country, along the lower valley of the Yellow River. Here too, the soil was enriched with the alluvium spread over the land by the floods. Probably this civilization goes back almost as far as those of Sumer and Egypt. However, we have no detailed information until about 1750 B.C., when the Shang dynasty kings began ruling China.

One of the capitals of the Shang dynasty has been excavated near the modern town of Anyang. This city was called by its inhabitants 'Great Shang', and was about half a mile long and a quarter of a mile wide. It was a planned city, with a royal palace and many upper-class houses. The houses were built of wood, and had gabled roofs supported on rows of pillars.

At Anyang, the tombs of some of the great Shang kings have been excavated. These kings were buried in a most unpleasant and grisly way that reminds us of the burials given to the early kings of Ur. A huge square pit was dug. From the middle of each side of the pit, gently sloping ramps were made, so that, seen from above, the grave looked rather like a cross. The royal coffin was placed in the centre of the pit. Then around it, and also along the ramps were laid the bodies of dozens of human victims and horses. These unfortunate men and animals had been slaughtered so that they could accompany their king to the next world.

The greatness of 'Great Shang' depended ultimately on the fertile countryside which surrounded it. Here there were many farming villages where barley, millet and rice were cultivated. Farmers kept pigs, cattle, sheep and goats, as well as water-buffaloes and chickens. Probably, too, the silkworm was already kept, and its thread woven into silken cloth.

Craftsmen of the Shang dynasty included carpenters and stone-carvers, potters (who had learned the use of the potter's wheel) and highly skilled bronze-smiths.

Many techniques, such as farming, bronze-working and the painting of pottery, are thought not to have developed in China, but to have spread there from the Near East. However this is not certain.

Above: jade hairpin in the form of a cock. Jade is a hard green, blue or white stone, much used by the Chinese for making ornamental objects. The angular design is characteristic of Shang Chinese style.

Right: two jade geese and a fish. These were amulets or charms, intended to ward off evil spirits. In Shang China it was the custom to bury them with the dead.

89

Left: a bronze wine vessel in the form of two rams, back to back. Such vessels were used in sacrificial rites to offer drinks to gods and spirits.

Below: Chinese writing. If you copy some of the characters you will realize that the modern ones are generally quicker to make than their ancient counterparts. It was the Chinese who, in the 2nd century A.D., invented true paper (as distinct from Egyptian-style papyrus).

	ancient	modern
goat, sheep	𐃮	羊
tree	木	木
field	田	田
earth	土	土
heaven	天	天
to pray	示	祝

In any case, from the very beginning, whatever China borrowed she quickly made her own. That is why the many works of art left behind by this civilization are so entirely different in style and feeling from anything we have met before.

The bronze vessels and other castings from the Shang dynasty are particularly admired for their perfection and beauty.

Entirely Chinese also was their system of writing. The origin of this is unknown, but the earliest examples have been found in the Shang dynasty tombs. At first the writing was carved on bones, but later the scribes used a brush on silk. This enabled them to paint their signs with such grace and charm that a piece of Chinese writing is almost a work of art. Originally the script included over 3,500 characters. The chart on the right shows that the same basic system of writing is still used in China today, where even now an alphabet has not been introduced.

Seal of a Cretan ship from Knossos.

Crete

In modern times 'Western civilization' has come to dominate the world. Yet it will now be clear that civilization did not begin in the west. At the time when the civilizations of Sumer and Egypt were flourishing, the people of western Europe had only recently learned the art of farming. They were still using stone tools and living in primitive huts. They did not learn the use of bronze until about 2000 B.C., and civilization was another 2,000 years in reaching them.

This new way of life advanced much more slowly to the west than to the east. We can best think of the westward advance of civilization as taking place in three stages. First it spread to Crete; next to Greece; finally it was brought to western Europe by the Romans. The first of these stages we must now consider.

A glance at the map below will show that the island of Crete provided a natural stepping stone between the civilizations of the Near East and the backward peoples of Europe; and it was Crete which became the home of the first European civilization.

We cannot be sure to what extent the rise of the Indian and Chinese civilizations depended on the direct influence of Sumer and Egypt. In the case of Crete, however, archaeologists have proved that the island was first colonized, about 5000 B.C., by peoples from western Asia. We also know that, about 3000 B.C., Egyptian settlers arrived bringing new ideas to this small and isolated country in the midst of the sea. At a later stage still, the trading interests of the Cretans kept them in constant touch with the progress being made in Egypt and other advanced lands.

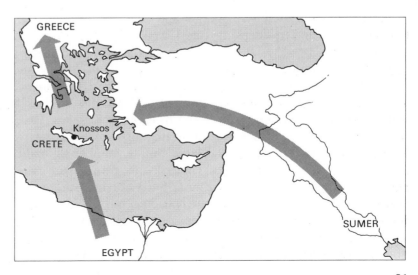

The spread of civilization from the Near East to Crete and then to Greece.

So we can be sure that the Cretans learned much from abroad. But for all that, they created a civilization which was different in many ways from the others we have discussed: a civilization which was original and peculiar to themselves.

Not many ancient legends are altogether true; on the other hand, not many are complete 'fairy stories'. Very often they contain a kernel of truth. So at least it has proved with the famous legend of Theseus and the Minotaur.

This was a tale told in Greece long after the Cretan civilization had been destroyed and forgotten. According to the legend, every nine years the Greek city of Athens had to send seven youths and seven maidens to Crete as a tribute. When these unhappy people arrived they were thrown into a labyrinth where a terrible monster called the Minotaur, half man and half bull, killed and devoured them. This sacrifice continued until Theseus, a prince of Athens, embarked with the victims and succeeded in killing the monster.

The ancient Greeks themselves believed Theseus to have been an historical figure who ruled Athens during the Mycenaean period (see chapter 7). But apart from this they had little idea to what past happenings this far-fetched story referred. It was not until modern times, when the renowned archaeologist, Sir Arthur Evans, discovered the remains of the palace at Knossos, that people realized there might be some truth in the Minotaur legend.

Theseus killing the Minotaur, as shown on a Greek pottery vessel of the classical period.

A labyrinth is an extremely complicated place with many passages, and one which is therefore hard, without guidance, to find your way through. On excavation, the plan of the palace at Knossos proved to be so elaborate and complicated that to the Greek youths and maidens it could well have seemed like a labyrinth.

Furthermore, the word Minotaur means 'bull of Minos' and Sir Arthur Evans discovered that the people of Crete were indeed keen on a daring and unusual form of bull-baiting. Wild bulls were captured out in the country and brought to Knossos. Here, with thousands of excited spectators watching, a bull was turned loose into a large arena. At the same time a number of highly trained girl and boy athletes entered the ring. They were absolutely unprotected and unarmed. Soon the bull charged at one of them. But, quite unfrightened, the boy or girl would stand motionless and watch it come. As the beast thundered in, at just the right instant, the athlete would grip the bull by the horns and lightly somersault over its back. Meanwhile a second athlete would come up behind the bull to catch the first as he bounced off, and so break his fall. All this can be seen in the famous bull-ring fresco (or wall painting) from Knossos (see below).

The idea of the game seems to have been for the young athletes to keep tormenting the bull in this dangerous way until eventually it was completely exhausted. Then perhaps the king himself would enter the ring and put an end to the defeated animal with his long bronze sword.

That at least is what would happen if highly skilled athletes were used, who had been trained for the job. But what might happen if those poor Greek youths and maidens were made to enter the ring? Without knowledge of the game, or proper training, until the heroic act of Theseus, they must have been killed by the bull. Was this, then, the kernel of truth in the Minotaur legend?

It is because of Crete's connexion with the Minotaur, and because the king of Crete was called the Minos, that this civilization is known as the Minoan civilization. It flourished for over a thousand years, from about 2500 to 1400 B.C.

'Bull-ring' fresco, showing youths and girls somersaulting over the bull's back.

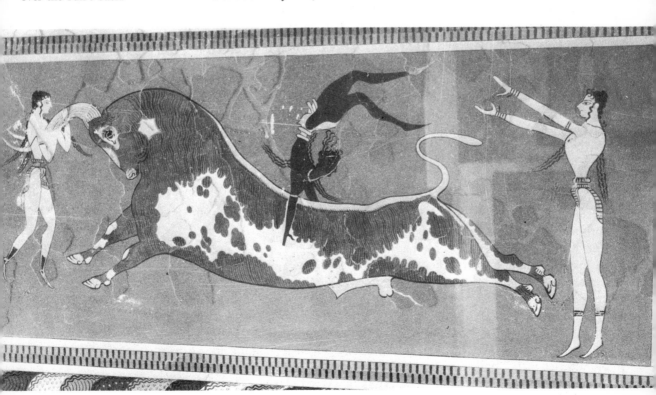

Left: part of the palace of Minos, Knossos, seen from the outside.

Below: a fresco at Knossos of a youth walking in the palace garden. Some people think the flowers are irises. The youth wears a short loin-cloth held in place by a broad belt, possibly of metal.

The palace of Minos at Knossos was an amazing building. It was roughly square, measuring about 450 feet each way. In the centre was a large open court. The ground-floor rooms on the western side were devoted to religious rites and ceremonies; for the kings of Crete, like those of Sumer, were priest-kings. Behind these rooms was a long corridor, with rows of storage chambers filled with jars of oil and corn. The whole of the first-floor storey above this western part of the palace formed the state apartments, lavishly decorated with fresco paintings on the walls.

On the eastern side of the court were the actual living quarters of the king and his family. These occupied two floors and were approached by the Grand Staircase made of broad stone steps. The king's and queen's bedrooms both had their own toilets and bathrooms attached. At Knossos full-size earthenware bathtubs were used, and there were modern water-closets linked to a drainage system that was even more remarkable than that at Mohenjo-daro.

In many parts of the palace, the walls were painted with scenes which depicted the life of the court: a youth walking in the garden; the bull-leaping game; the palace ladies, dressed in almost modern costume, performing a sacred dance. These

Drawing of the 'ladies in blue' fresco. This is among the finest Minoan wall paintings. The ladies wear short-sleeved jackets. The hair-styles, though basically the same, differ slightly from one another.

Drawing of a Cretan house plaque. Note the many windows: this was a Cretan innovation, as the sun was less intense than in Mesopotamia and Egypt.

pictures were in delightful colours, and still quiver with vitality and movement. They show not only that the Minoans were an artistic people, but also that they lived a very free, gay and happy social life. Indeed the Minoan civilization has been called 'one of the most graceful civilizations the world has ever seen'.

The great palace at Knossos looked down on a town of brick-built houses, where about 100,000 people lived. Immediately surrounding the palace was a residential quarter containing the homes of the nobles and wealthy merchants. Beyond this, towards the edge of the city, lived the traders and craftsmen in smaller and poorer houses. As you will see from the illustration on the left, a Minoan house was not so very different from those we live in today. It was two or three storeys high, and had very modern-looking doors and windows.

Knossos was the greatest Minoan city, but there were many others. The island was known as 'hundred-citied Crete'. There were also hundreds of small towns and villages, so it was a very thickly populated country indeed.

One result of this was that the farmlands could not possibly grow enough corn to support all the townsfolk and provide the wealth needed to build their cities. This was even more true since there was a shortage of good farming land in Crete. The Minoan civilization is the first we have discussed which did not have a rich and fertile river valley or an irrigation system.

Clearly, the Minoans could not rely merely on farming for their prosperity. More than any other ancient people, they had to make and sell things. Nor was it enough to sell goods at home. They needed to export. The wealth of the Minoans largely depended on overseas trade. The position of their towns proves this, for all the great cities are near the coast. Inland there are only small towns and villages.

What did the Cretans make and sell? They kept large numbers of sheep, and wove the wool into cloth. Their craftsmen worked in ivory, gold, silver and bronze. But still more famous were the potters. They made vessels of every size and for every purpose. There were delicate cups, as thin-walled and exquisite as those of a modern china tea-service. At the other extreme were giant vases and storage jars, as tall as a man. Whatever their size these vessels were always attractively shaped and decorated. Cretan potters were particularly fond of designs based on nature. They loved painting birds, or the slender stalks of plants as they swayed in the breeze. Or else they copied things that they found in the sea: shells, starfish, seaweed, and the long tentacles of the octopus.

Such pottery, like the work of the Cretan metal-smiths and other craftsmen, was exported all over the eastern Mediterranean: to Egypt, Syria, Cyprus, the Aegean Islands, Greece, Italy, Sicily. In some of these countries, permanent trading posts were founded. Egyptian records show that the Minoans sold to Egypt ingots of bronze, splendid cups and bowls made of precious metals, and pottery vases filled with the finest quality olive oil. They took back to Crete papyrus, linen, ivory, gold and spices.

Another important thing which these Egyptian records tell us is that the goods which passed between the two countries were carried by Cretan ships; and no doubt the same applied to most of the cargoes going to and from other lands. In their high-prowed boats, the Minoan sailors are thought to have been the first who were daring enough to regularly sail across the 'Great Green', as the Egyptians called the open Mediterranean.

Thus Crete became a great trading country, and the first major sea-power known to history. In these, as in many other ways, this earliest European civilization seems quite different from those of Sumer and Egypt. In fact we can recognize it as distinctly related to our own.

The Minoans developed two entirely different types of writing. The first was a hieroglyphic script, or form of picture-writing. But later they devised another script based on syllables, which is known as Linear A (see illustration opposite). Not surprisingly, perhaps, they seem to have written chiefly for business purposes. So, unlike the Sumerians and the Egyptians, the Cretans left no works of learning or literature.

Above: a giant storage jar over 6 feet high, still stands among the ruins of a Minoan city.

Below: a flask on which is painted an octopus. The pot is cream in colour with decoration in dark green.

96

Dates to remember

from about 2500 to 1500 B.C. The Indus Valley civilization

1750 B.C. The Shang dynasty begins

from about 2500 to 1400 B.C. The Minoan civilization

Things to discuss

Which of the first five civilizations would you prefer to have lived in?

Things to do

1 Make the ancient and modern Chinese characters shown on page 86 with a brush, using either paint or ink. Are the ancient or the modern characters easier to make? Why is this?
2 Describe an imaginary visit to Mohenjo-daro.
3 Study the pictures of as many Minoan pots as you can. Then design a pot of your own, using the Cretan style.
4 In addition to the palace at Knossos, another great Minoan palace has been excavated at Phaistos. Find out something about this, and say whether it was similar to the palace at Knossos, or not.
5 We have only discussed the development of civilization in the Old World. From other books find out what you can about one of the civilizations of the New World, i.e. the Olmec, Mayan or Peruvian civilizations.

Books to read

E. Royston Pike, *Ancient India*, Weidenfeld & Nicolson

L. Cottrell, *The Bull of Minos*, Cadet edition, Evans

G. L. Field, *The Minoans of Ancient Crete*, Wheaton

R. Fawcett, *Crete*, Gawthorn

Below: hieroglyphic script, in use from about 2000 B.C. Some of the pictographic signs were borrowed from Egypt, but the majority were devised by the Cretans themselves.
Below right: Linear A script which developed from the hieroglyphic script and had replaced it by about 1600 B.C.

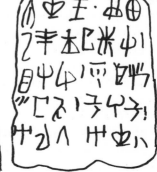

Chapter 6
How new peoples destroyed the old civilizations

The story of how in the space of a few thousand years the hunts-man became first a farmer and then a city-dweller has been described as 'the greatest story in the history of man'. And, indeed, perhaps nothing that has happened since is quite so remarkable as this crucial move forward from cave-life to civilization.

The beginnings of this vital advance took place in the early farming settlements of south-western Asia, such as Jericho. Then came the great civilizations of Sumer, Egypt, India, China, and Crete.

Though these civilizations may sometimes have borrowed ideas from one another, each can truly be called an original civilization. All of them started from scratch: with primitive village settlements surrounded by untamed marsh and desert and waste. The imposing cities, the fine palaces and temples which they built were due to their own inventiveness and creative effort.

For the most part, such progress had taken place in peaceful and settled conditions. But we now come to a stage in man's story which is full of unrest, the swift movement of new peoples into the old centres of civilization. For the first time, what must chiefly concern us is war and conquest. One after another, the old civilizations allowed themselves to be defeated and taken over by backward, uncivilized peoples. Often the old states were at loggerheads within, or else they had become too soft and easy-going as a result of their wealth and prosperity. The invaders, on the other hand, though they were less clever, were tough and vigorous and determined.

The first of the original civilizations to be overcome in this way was the first which had been created, Sumer. We ended chapter 3 by explaining how the Sumerians lived in constant fear of backward tribes on both sides of them.

Presumed head of Sargon, excavated at Ninevah. He looks like a typical Semitic sheik, with high cheek-bones, an aquiline nose and soft curly beard.

The fertile lands

Throughout ancient times many peoples of south-western Asia found themselves faced by a double threat of this kind. The reason was that in this part of the world there is a shortage of good farming land. To the north and east the country is barren and mountainous; to the south all is desert.

The peoples who at any time occupied the fertile lands were looked upon with great jealousy by the nomadic peoples on either side. Indeed if these settled folk, in their wealthy cities, showed the slightest sign of weakness, they were almost certain to be attacked and overcome, either from the highlands, or else by tribes coming out of the desert.

The wandering tribes who threatened from the Syrian and Arabian deserts were all of Semitic blood; that is to say they were the ancestors of the Arab and the Jew. At first, the main danger, as far as Sumer was concerned, came from a Semitic people called the Akkadians.

The Semitic invasions and the first empire

These uncivilized nomads began by nudging their way into Mesopotamia to the north of the Sumerians. They thus occupied an area which became known after them as Akkad. But about 2400 B.C., under their leader Sargon, the Akkadian armies swept down into Sumer itself. One after another the Sumerian city-states were defeated and forced to submit to foreign rule.

Nor was this enough for Sargon. With scarcely a pause, he led his swift-moving archers into Elam, a mountainous country beyond the river Tigris. Then, having captured Elam, he turned and marched northwards up the Euphrates, conquering as he went, until eventually he had won an empire which stretched from the shores of the Mediterranean to the Persian Gulf. Sargon thereby became the first man in history to make an empire.

What do we mean by this word 'empire'? It is a territory ruled by one man or one government. In this it is like a nation. But whereas a nation consists of one country, an empire includes several different countries, and is usually made by one people conquering others and forcing them into submission and servitude.

Sargon's empire was the first of many which came into being – and also disappeared – during this phase in our story. For 2,000 years, the same changes seem to take place everywhere. Warlike barbarian tribes move into the old civilized lands. They conquer the original inhabitants and take over their wealth and their cities. But the original inhabitants are not put to death or driven out. They are simply made to acknowledge the newcomers as lords and masters; they have to work for them, becoming subject peoples. Otherwise life goes on much as before.

Clay tablet showing an outline map of the regions of the world. The cuneiform writing tells of the conquests of Sargon. The tablet was made about 600 B.C. in Babylonia, and proves that the feats of this first Semitic emperor were long remembered.

Laws of Hammurabi. The pillar which is nearly 8 feet high contains over 3,600 lines of cuneiform writing. The Babylonian Sun god is seated on the right and holds in his outstretched hand the measuring-rod and line, symbols of justice and straightforward dealing. Comparison with the similar scene on pages 48–9 shows how closely Hammurabi was following an ancient Sumerian tradition.

In fact, a rather unexpected thing frequently happens when a backward people conquers a highly civilized race. Eventually it is the conquered people who prove to have done the real conquering. For the uncouth newcomers, though at first they may despise the subject race, soon discover many things they cannot help but respect and admire. In the course of time, they drop many of their own primitive ideas and practices, and take over the civilized ways of the conquered peoples. In the desert, Sargon's Akkadians had been tent-dwellers, but it was not long before they discovered that they preferred living in houses. In the desert they had known nothing of writing; yet once they had come down into Sumer, they were soon learning to write with cuneiform signs. So it was that the ideas of the vanquished proved stronger than the armies of the victors, and after the Akkadian take-over a mixed Semitic and Sumerian state soon emerged, which carried on very much in the original Sumerian tradition.

About 1750 B.C. a Semitic leader named Hammurabi became king of the Mesopotamian empire, which was henceforward known as Babylonia. Hammurabi was a highly efficient organizer, and was determined to see that order was kept and justice done throughout his empire. He therefore collected together many of the ancient laws and customs, both of his own Semitic people, and of the Sumerians. Then he arranged them systematically, adding to them where necessary, and had this 'code', or collection of almost 300 laws, carved on a large pillar of stone (see opposite). The cuneiform writing runs right round the column, and above it Hammurabi himself is depicted standing reverently in front of the Babylonian Sun god to show that his code was in accordance with the will of heaven.

The basic idea behind many of the laws was that of straight-forward revenge or retaliation: 'An eye for an eye, a tooth for a tooth'. Here is an example:

If a man has caused the loss of a gentleman's eye, his own eye one shall cause to be lost. If he has shattered a gentleman's limb, one shall shatter his limb.

But there appears to have been one law for the rich and another for the poor in Hammurabi's Babylonia as may be seen from the next law, which reads:

If he has caused a poor man to lose his eye or shattered a poor man's limb, he shall pay one *mina* of silver.

Today we would consider the 'money' fine of the second law a much more humane and civilized punishment than the brutal retaliatory justice of the first. On the other hand, the idea of some people being 'worth' more than others seems quite wrong by modern standards.

For all its shortcomings, however, Hammurabi's code is a noteworthy landmark in human progress. Laws are essential to civilized societies, and it is important that they should be written down so that people have no doubt as to what is, and what is not, wrong. Although parts of earlier codes have survived, Hammurabi's is the oldest complete law code that is known to us. Another reason these laws are important is that, through Moses, their 'eye for an eye' principle later passed into the law of the Hebrew people, as you can see by looking up Exodus, chapter XXI, verses 23–25.

By the time of Hammurabi, the second oldest civilization, ancient Egypt, had also been taken over by Semites, drifting up from the southern desert. These Egyptian Semites were called the Hyksos. We do not know a great deal about them, but it seems that they ruled the land of the Pharaohs for about 200 years, from 1750 to 1550 B.C.

The Indo-European invasions – first wave

Meanwhile another danger had begun to threaten the cradle-lands of civilization. From about 2000 B.C. hordes of uncivilized peoples, even tougher and more highly skilled in war than the Semites, were pressing down from the highland zone in the north.

These northern invaders were all members of a race known as Indo-Europeans. Their original home was in the wide steppe-lands of south Russia. They were a restless nomadic people, who kept herds of horses and were constantly on the move in search of fresh pasture for them. It was on the newly domesticated horse that their power largely depended, for they fought in horse-drawn battle-chariots. These chariots had light wooden frames covered by leather- or basket-work, and ran on spoked wheels. Each was drawn by two horses, harnessed to a central pole, so they were extremely swift-moving vehicles. In battle, each chariot carried a driver, and a warrior who fought with a bow or spear.

Only the Indo-Europeans had horse-drawn chariots at this time. Once they began moving into south-western Asia, therefore, the settled peoples had no defence against them.

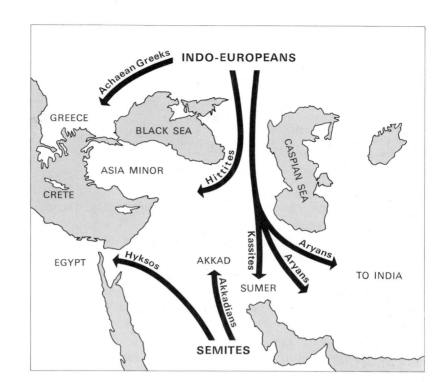

The first wave of invasions (from about 2400 to 1400 B.C.). The Kassites defeated the Semites soon after the time of Hammurabi, and gained control of much of Mesopotamia.

A Hittite chariot. Compare it with the Sumerian chariots shown on the 'Royal Standard' of Ur (page 52).

Like the Semitic invaders from the south, the Indo-Europeans came in several different groups. The first to arrive were the Hittites. Before 2000 B.C., they were fighting their way through the gap between the Black Sea and the Caspian. By 1700 B.C., they were creating a large and powerful empire based on Asia Minor.

The invention of iron

It may have been the Hittites who made one of the few important discoveries of this period, the smelting of iron. Unlike bronze, which was always rare and costly, iron soon became plentiful and cheap. Unhappily, to begin with, most of it went into the making of cheaper and more deadly weapons, so that by helping armies to become bigger and better equipped, it only made these warlike times still more frightening and terrible.

On the other hand, this invention also made cheap metal tools possible for the first time. Ultimately this was of enormous benefit to farmers, carpenters, and many other craftsmen; and so to mankind in general.

The way in which the new inventions that man makes can be used either for good or for evil purposes is something we cannot help noticing, not only in the past, but in our own times, with the discovery of such things as atomic power.

Historians call the period which was dominated by the use of iron the Iron Age, just as we sometimes refer to our own age as the Atomic Age. The Bronze Age came to its close and the Iron Age began round about 1200 B.C. in the Near East. But, as with bronze before it, it was only slowly that the use of iron spread to other parts of the world.

The Aryans and Achaean Greeks

Closely following the Hittites came more Indo-European peoples. Among the most important were the Aryans who, in about 1500 B.C., attacked India and the Indus Valley civilization, which seemed to have been declining rapidly at that time.

Then there were the Achaean or Mycenaean Greeks who entered eastern Europe and conquered the whole of the Greek peninsula. Though it is not known for certain, some historians think that later these Mycenaeans crossed to Crete and captured Knossos.

Thus, at about the same time as the Indus Valley civilization was being destroyed in the east, the western Minoan civilization also suffered a mortal defeat.

An iron arrow-head and an iron sickle blade. Both were made by the Assyrians (see page 101) in about the 7th century B.C.

A Hittite captain holding what is probably an iron-tipped spear. This is part of a wall found at the city of Carchemish dated about 900 B.C.

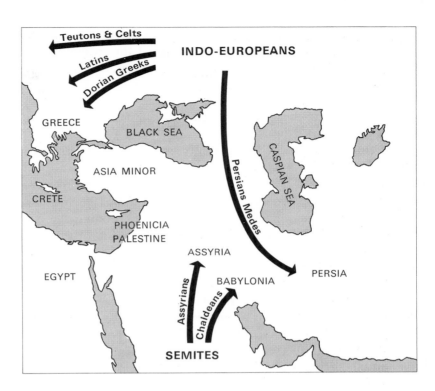

The second wave of invasions
(from about 1200 B.C.).

The second wave of invasions

So ended one wave of invasions. But before long a second wave followed – both from the south and north. Out of the desert came first the Assyrians and then the Chaldeans.

The armies of Assyria dominated Mesopotamia from the 12th century B.C. until 612 B.C. After this, from 612 to 538 B.C., the Chaldeans ruled a large empire from Babylon.

But the Semites were not to remain the ruling race in Mesopotamia for ever. Starting about 1200 B.C. new hordes of Indo-Europeans began moving in from the highlands. Now these frightful northern invaders had discarded their chariots. The stirrup had been invented, so they rode into battle astride their horses.

Soon the Medes and Persians conquered Iran, which was henceforth known as Persia. Then they overran Mesopotamia, capturing the Chaldean-Babylonian empire in 538 B.C. Nor did they rest content until they had added Egypt and Asia Minor to their dominions, thereby becoming masters of the whole Near and Middle East. The creation of this empire meant the final victory of the northern Indo-Europeans over the southern Semites.

It was a colossal task to govern such a vast area, and the highly efficient system of organization which the Persians developed ranks among the outstanding achievements of the ancient world. The ultimate source of all authority and power was the Great King, whose word was law and to whom everyone in the empire owed absolute obedience. However, as long as the subject peoples accepted this fact, they were treated with humanity and justice by their conquerors.

The empire was divided into twenty provinces (satrapies) each under the rule of a governor (satrap), who was generally a member of the royal house or a great noble. The governors were responsible for looking after all matters affecting the life and welfare of their particular province, as well as running the law courts, collecting the imperial taxes and feeding the royal garrisons.

It was essential that the king should be fully informed of what was happening in the various parts of the empire, and that his commands should be conveyed to every quarter with the utmost speed. So the Persians built a remarkable network of roads which linked the far-flung provinces to the capital. For the purpose of conveying official messages they also created a postal service. This meant having a chain of hostels at regular intervals along each of the main roads, from which royal messengers were ready to ride at any hour of the day or night with imperial despatches. Such places also provided lodging and refreshment for other travellers.

A Persian archer from the palace of Susa built in about 490 B.C. by Darius I. The archer carries his bow over his left shoulder.

For about two centuries this Persian system of administration brought a high standard of peace, order and justice to the Near and Middle East. Just as important, it set an example to the Macedonians and Romans who later adopted similar methods in running their own empires.

The Persians had an interesting religion which was based on the teachings of a great prophet named Zarathustra. He insisted that there was only one good god, Ahura Mazdah, 'the lord who knows'. Opposed to him, however, was an evil spirit named Ahriman. According to Zarathustra everybody in the world was caught up in the titanic struggle which was forever raging between these two. People who lived a virtuous life were helping the good god; those who lied, cheated or made others unhappy were allying themselves to the evil spirit.

In other ways the Persians were less creative and original. They had little interest in learning and made few inventions or discoveries. Apart from religious texts and countless inscriptions glorifying their kings, they left no literature. Their art and architecture were impressive, but depended mainly on the ideas and skills of the conquered peoples and other non-Persians.

Turning now to Europe, with the second wave of Indo-Europeans came the Dorian Greeks. They defeated their predecessors, the Mycenaean Greeks, and totally destroyed their cities.

Meanwhile, still other Indo-Europeans who were later to play an important part in history – the Latins, the Teutons and the Celts – were overrunning much of the rest of Europe.

On the whole, then, the period of nearly 2,000 years, from 2400 B.C., when the first Semites conquered Sumer, to 500 B.C., and the last ravages of the Indo-Europeans, was a destructive rather than a creative period. It was an age of much fighting but of little progress; of large empires but small achievements.

Nevertheless, both the Semite and the Indo-European races had important parts to play in the development of Western civilization.

The great empires of the Semites, if they added comparatively few new ideas, at least preserved the original heritage; and later peoples found they had much to learn from them. Two tiny Semitic peoples, the Phoenicians and the Hebrews, had an influence on the future which was out of proportion to their numbers.

The Phoenicians

Originally the Phoenicians had dwelt in the desert. But, in the course of time, they managed to win a home for themselves along the eastern shore of the Mediterranean. This was just to the north of Palestine, in a land which was sometimes known as Phoenicia and sometimes (as it is today) as Lebanon.

In the desert the Phoenicians had lived a wandering life. When they arrived in Lebanon they adopted more settled ways and quickly became town-dwellers. Yet they remained wanderers too. Before, they had wandered endlessly over the sands on their camels. Now they took to ships and began to wander endlessly across the sea.

At first, it is true, they were much less important as traders and seamen than the Minoans and the Mycenaean Greeks. For one thing, in their single-masted ships, they kept timidly to the coasts and refused to venture out into the open Mediterranean. Down to about 1200 B.C., most of their trade was with Egypt which they could reach by following their own shoreline southwards.

But then the Minoan and Mycenaean civilizations were destroyed and the 'Great Green' became suddenly empty of shipping. This was a marvellous opportunity for the Phoenicians and they seized it eagerly. By 1000 B.C. they had made themselves into skilful and courageous navigators and were bartering their wares in every part of the eastern Mediterranean.

Nor did these dark-headed traders stop there. Soon they sailed into the western Mediterranean, and even through the Straits of Gibraltar into the Atlantic Ocean, where the Minoans had never ventured.

As a result of this extensive seafaring and trade, Phoenician cities along the Lebanese coast, like Byblos, Tyre and Sidon, became fabulously wealthy. Wherever they went the Phoenicians founded colonies. Some were only small trading posts, but others became thriving cities in their own right and one grew to be still more influential and wealthy than those in Phoenicia itself. This was the city of Carthage on the north coast of Africa, which we shall speak of again later.

The Phoenicians were not merely traders; they had skilled craftsmen and artists, capable of manufacturing all sorts of things. From early times they had been famous for a purple dye which only they could produce. This was made from a shell-fish found along the Lebanese coast, and elsewhere in the Mediterranean, called the murex. The fine linen garments which the Phoenicians dyed in this purple were very popular everywhere

Phoenician influence. The tin route went as far north as the Scilly Isles. In the 5th century B.C., a Carthaginian, Hanno, travelled down the west coast of Africa.

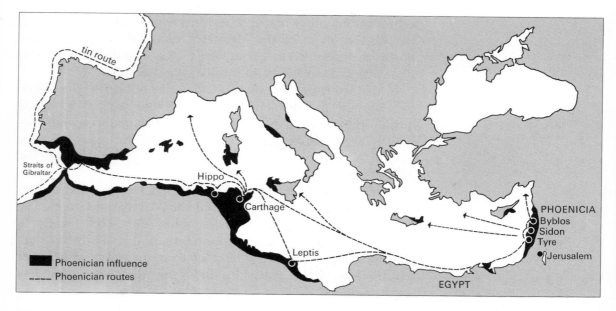

Phoenician ships. The smaller ones, with tall vertical prow and stern, are trading vessels; the larger ones are war-galleys. Both types have a raised deck and two banks of oars. Both types were fitted with a single mast, but in this relief carving only the war-galleys are shown with their masts in position. This is a drawing from an Assyrian low relief carving.

The Phoenician harbour of Byblos, as it looks today. Because much of the papyrus used by the Greeks came from here, they often called it *'byblos'*. Later when the Greeks began writing books on rolls of paper they called them *'biblia'*, and we get the word Bible from this term.

Left: Phoenician vessels of coloured glass, which the Phoenicians learnt how to make from the Egyptians. According to the Roman writer Pliny, transparent glass was invented by chance in Phoenicia when blocks of saltpetre were being burned in contact with sand on the shore.

Below: a Phoenician gold ear-ring, with hawk and vase pendants. (The top is missing.)

their traders called. The Phoenicians were also highly capable workers in ivory and bronze. Then, having learned the art of making glass from the Egyptians, they were soon selling their own attractive glassware throughout the Mediterranean world.

It cannot be stressed too strongly how important international trade has always been in the history of civilization. When traders like the Phoenicians travelled over wide areas, it was not merely goods and merchandise that passed from people to people. Ideas and the knowledge of new inventions were passed on as well. Thus the backward countries, in addition to buying things, were always *learning* things from the Phoenicians.

Over the centuries countless valuable ideas must have been spread from place to place in this way. But one idea was of particular importance. This was the 'priceless gift' of alphabetic writing.

We have already traced the story of writing through the early stages of its development. The first stage was simple picture-writing. In the second stage, the signs were no longer pictures, but stood for spoken syllables. Up to this point, the Sumerians had led the way, but the Egyptians must have the

Egyptian	𓃾	〜
early Phoenician	⊁	4
late Greek	ᐊ	N
Latin	A	N
English	A	N

Two of the 22 letters in the Phoenician alphabet with their equivalents in Egyptian, Greek, Latin and English. See if you can find the whole alphabet in a reference book and make a copy of it.

credit for the third advance. They had about twenty-four characters which stood, not for syllables, but for simple sounds; in other words, twenty-four true letters. However, the Egyptians failed to realize that it would be possible to write using only these alphabetic letters, so their script continued to be complicated by many hundreds of other signs.

It was either the Phoenicians themselves, or else some nearby Semitic people who were responsible for the fourth stage. The effect which this advance had on writing was of immense importance. Yet, in a sense, it was the easiest and most obvious development of all. It simply meant realizing what the Egyptians had failed to appreciate: that their few alphabetic signs were enough by themselves. With these alone, using each letter to stand for a simple sound, every word could be spelt out.

Perhaps the Phoenicians were not the people who made this discovery. But they certainly wasted little time in adopting it for writing their own language. The illustration (*left*) shows how the Phoenician signs came originally from Egypt and were subsequently handed down to us through the Greeks and the Romans.

Memorizing the alphabet was greatly helped by the fact that each letter had a name and was placed in a fixed order. The first letter was called 'aleph', which meant 'ox'; the second was called 'beth', meaning 'house'. When children repeated their letters they began 'aleph', 'beth'; and that is where the word 'alphabet' comes from.

In early times, because of the complicated nature of the scripts, writing had been confined to priests and other privileged classes. But the ease with which the alphabet could be learned changed all this. Now there was no reason why quite ordinary people should not read and write.

So the Phoenician alphabet spread eastwards to India; westwards to Greece, and then to the rest of Europe. Every alphabet in the civilized world has descended from it.

The Phoenician alphabet had only one disadvantage. Like the Egyptian, it had no signs for vowels, only for consonants. It was the Greeks who spotted this defect, and so made the final advance (stage five) towards a complete system of alphabetic writing, by adding the necessary vowel signs.

At first the Phoenicians wrote on clay tablets, like the Sumerians; but they soon changed over to the Egyptian idea of using pen, ink and papyrus. So, as their merchants sailed about the Mediterranean, they introduced into other lands, not only the alphabet, but also the things which we still use for writing it.

The Hebrews

The other small Semitic people who have had a great influence on the history of Western civilization are the Hebrews. Like the Phoenicians, the Hebrews were originally nomads of the Arabian desert, who later found their way into the fertile lands of south-western Asia. But, as with the Phoenicians, this was far from being the end of their wanderings.

Abraham, the patriarch or father of the Jewish race, seems to have been settled at Ur in Sumer about 1900 B.C. Here, although publicly he had to pay tribute to Nannar, the city's moon god, privately he continued to worship the god of his own family and people. It was this 'Lord' who 'said unto Abram, Get thee out of thy country . . . unto a land that I will shew thee. And I will make of thee a great nation.'

Abraham responded to that call, and in the shepherd wanderings which followed, he and his family were led to Canaan, where God had promised them a 'land flowing with milk and honey'. Ultimately, this and the previous promise were fulfilled; but it was many hundreds of years after the death of Abraham.

During this interval the children of Israel had to endure a long period of 'captivity' in Egypt. And even when Moses led them out of that land, they still had ahead another forty years of wandering in the wilderness or desert. Eventually, however, under the leadership of Joshua, the twelve tribes of the Hebrews, as they had now become, managed to gain a foothold in Canaan or Palestine. And here, under their kings, Saul, David and Solomon, and amidst much fighting, they finally achieved nationhood.

Solomon's reign saw the building of the Temple at Jerusalem (see First Book of Kings, chapter 6). In comparison with similar buildings elsewhere in the ancient world, this was neither large, nor particularly magnificent. Nevertheless, the opening of the Temple was an event of far-reaching importance since, as the central shrine of the Jews, it became a symbol of all that they stood for.

Yet after the fulfilment of this national dream, and the death of Solomon, the Hebrews fell out among themselves. Henceforth they were divided into two nations: the kingdom of Judah in the south, with its capital at Jerusalem, and the kingdom of Israel in the north.

About 700 B.C. Israel was conquered by the Assyrians and its people were transported to a remote part of the Assyrian empire, thereby becoming the 'ten lost tribes of Israel'.

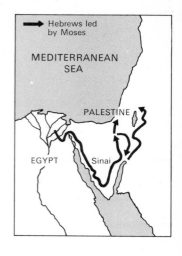

The desert wanderings of the Hebrews under Moses.

Part of the 'black obelisk' of Shalmaneser III, which shows Israelites bringing tribute to Shalmaneser, the Assyrian king. According to the cuneiform inscription, this consisted of 'silver, gold, golden bowls, a golden vase, golden vessels and buckets, a royal staff, and fruits'. The incident, which is not recorded in the Bible, occurred almost 150 years before Israel was finally conquered by the Assyrians.

Then in 597 B.C. Jerusalem itself was sacked by the Chaldean emperor Nebuchadnezzar. The temple was destroyed and the majority of the inhabitants of Judah were transported as captives to Babylon (Second Book of Kings, chapter 24).

But when Babylon in its turn was seized by the Persians, Cyrus allowed the Jews to return to their own land, where one of their first acts was to rebuild the Temple.

The whole of this long and dramatic story of the Hebrew people can be read, as they themselves recorded it, in the early books of the Old Testament. This is unquestionably one of the most amazing collections of writings which have been bequeathed to us by the ancient world; and, together with the New Testament, it has had a greater influence on our own Western civilization than any other book.

Some of the Old Testament stories are legendary, such as the accounts of the Creation and the Flood, which Abraham probably brought with him from Sumer (see page 49). Other stories, dealing with the history of the Hebrews, though they are undoubtedly based on truth, have become oversimplified and distorted by countless re-tellings before they were written down. All the same, it is impossible to read the Old Testament without sensing the unique qualities of the Hebrews.

Their claim on history does not rest on wealth and power, large armies and vast empires, but on an unshakeable faith that has survived from the Old Testament to the modern state of Israel. Amid their endless setbacks and tribulations, the Hebrews kept faith in their own God, the one true God, they called him, the God of Abraham, of Isaac and of Jacob. At first their idea of God was a primitive one. But gradually, as crisis followed crisis, under the leadership of their prophets, a less terrifying and more subtle idea of God emerged: the concept of God which is today the basis not only of Jewish religion but of much Christian teaching also. Thus the Hebrews laid the foundation of our own spiritual beliefs and of many of our ideas about goodness and right conduct.

The importance of the Indo-Europeans

Enough has now been said to make plain the importance of the Semitic race for the future of mankind. The importance of the Indo-European races can be seen by a glance at the map opposite, which shows us the spread of the Indo-European languages to almost every part of the globe.

Nor was it just languages and peoples which spread in this way. In India, the victorious Aryans adopted many of the ideas and beliefs of the defeated Indus Valley people. There was a mixture of old and new, and the resulting Hindu civilization is still the civilization of India today.

In Europe, the chief Indo-European contribution came at first from the Greeks. They learned much from the Minoans, the Egyptians and the Mesopotamian peoples. Then they added countless new ideas and enrichments of their own; and, together with the Semitic Hebrews, laid the foundations of our own Western civilization.

Dates to remember

about 2400 B.C.   Sargon conquers Sumer and makes the first great empire
from 2000 B.C.   First wave of Indo-European invasions
about 1900 B.C.   Abraham at Ur
from 1200 B.C.   Second wave of Indo-European invasions
960 B.C.   Completion of the Temple at Jerusalem

Things to do

1   From other books, find out about either the Assyrian or Chaldean empires. Make notes on the main achievements of the people you study. Do you agree that they did less to help forward the progress of mankind than the Sumerians or the Egyptians?

2   The Assyrians were famous for two things: war and art. Find out what you can about their art, particularly their sculpture. Make one or two drawings of Assyrian things.

3   Prepare a sketch map showing the positions of Phoenicia, Israel and Judah. Mark Jerusalem; also Byblos, Tyre and Sidon, and one or two other Phoenician cities.

4   The Assyrians conquered Israel, but not Judah. However, according to the Assyrian account, Hezekiah, King of Judah, was virtually defeated, and 'like a caged bird, shut up in Jerusalem'. Read the Second Book of Chronicles, chapter 32, verses 1–23. Then explain how the Hebrew account differs from the Assyrian one. Which do you think the more likely to be true, and why?

5   The earliest known Old Testament manuscripts are the Dead Sea Scrolls, believed by some scholars to date from the second century B.C. Try to discover more about them, and about the dramatic way they were found in 1947.

6   From about 1200 B.C., the peoples of the Near East entered what historians call the Iron Age. Make a list of the three earlier ages, keeping them in the correct order. If you add the Iron Age, this is a complete list of the main 'Ages' through which early man passed.

Books to read

H. W. F. Saggs, *Everyday Life in Babylonia and Assyria*, Batsford
E. W. Heaton, *Everyday Life in Old Testament Times*, Batsford

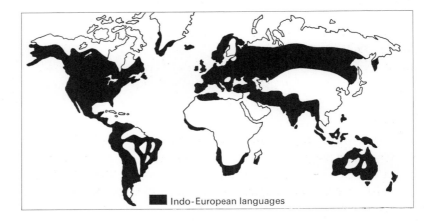

Areas where Indo-European languages are spoken. English, Spanish and Portuguese have largely replaced the native languages of North and South America.

Indo-European languages

Chapter 7
The first citizens: Greece

The Achaean Greeks

The first Greeks to settle in the country which still bears their name were the Achaean Greeks. They came from the north about 2000 B.C. with the first wave of chariot-riding Indo-Europeans.

These Achaeans must have been a primitive nomadic people when they arrived. However, they had entered a highly civilized world. To the east of the Greek peninsula is the Aegean Sea, which is cut off from the main part of the Mediterranean by the island of Crete. Here the Minoan civilization was at the height of its power; and in the course of time the Greeks – like all the other Aegean peoples – came under its influence.

Greece is a mountainous country with many valleys that run down to the sea. Generally the mountains separate the people of one valley from those of another. It was natural, therefore, that the Achaeans, instead of becoming a single nation, should find themselves divided into many small kingdoms: like Mycenae, Thebes, Athens and Sparta.

Every kingdom had a city at its centre where the main building was a royal palace. This stood on high ground and was surrounded by a strong defensive wall. Here the king and his nobles lived a life of great luxury and splendour. But, beyond the citadel walls, the peasants who tilled the fields counted for little more than slaves.

Citadel of Mycenae today. The lower town walls are from a much later date (3rd century B.C.).

Lion Gate at Mycenae, from the outside. Each lion rests its forepaws on an altar of traditional Cretan type, surmounted by a sacred column. The Lion Gate was set in position more than 3,000 years ago. Note the strength of the citadel walls.

The Mycenaean civilization

It was at Mycenae that the famous German archaeologist, Heinrich Schliemann, originally discovered the remains of this first Greek civilization; as a result historians speak of it as the Mycenaean civilization.

The Mycenaeans learned most of their ideas from the Minoans. Like them, they depended for their prosperity on the sea and trade. Their royal palaces were decorated in the Cretan style. Their art and pottery and metalwork were largely borrowed from Crete; so, too, was their system of writing.

But some things the Mycenaeans did not copy. They kept their own language and their own religion. Like other Indo-Europeans, they also kept their love of spoken poetry. The favourite

117

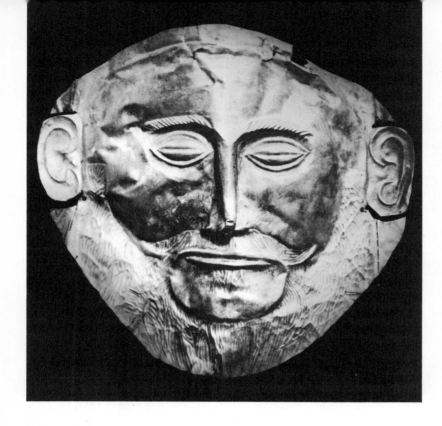

The golden mask from Mycenae. As a schoolboy, Heinrich Schliemann loved the *Iliad* of Homer (see page 116) which tells how Agamemnon, King of Mycenae, led the Greeks on the siege of Troy. When he found this mask of beaten gold Schliemann telegraphed home, 'I have looked upon the face of Agamemnon.' In fact the mask dates from several centuries earlier.

Below: Mycenean influence is believed to have spread as far as England: knowledge of the building techniques used at Stonehenge (see pages 174–5) may have come from Mycenae. This seems confirmed by the discovery in 1953 of a carving on one of the Stonehenge stones of a bronze dagger of the Mycenean type.

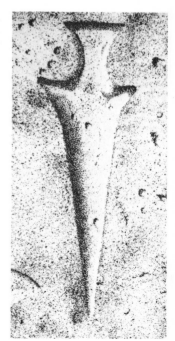

entertainment of the kings and nobles was to sit around in their palace halls and listen to a bard – or poet – reciting the epic stories of the Greek heroes and gods.

In the legend of Theseus and the Minotaur, the Greek city of Athens had to pay a regular tribute of seven youths and seven maidens to Crete. Probably this was one of the stories the bards told. It refers to a time when the Minoans were stronger than the Greeks and had control over their cities.

However, before 1400 B.C. that situation had been reversed; perhaps because the Mycenaeans had invaded Crete, captured Knossos, and brought to an end the civilization from which they had learned so much. For the next two centuries they themselves were the major power in the Aegean world. Everywhere the Minoan sailors had once sailed, the Mycenaeans sailed now. They carried their cargoes as far as Palestine and Egypt in the east, and as far as Sicily in the west.

These early Greeks were a warlike people and fond of adventure. Towards the end of the Mycenaean period, they quarrelled with a wealthy trading city in Asia Minor known as Troy. After a long siege, Troy was captured and burned to the ground.

The main Greek cities.

The Dorian invasions and the Dark Age

But not much later, the Mycenaean cities suffered a similar fate.

This sudden catastrophe was the work of the Dorians who swept furiously down into the Greek peninsula about 1200 B.C. Historians believe that the Dorians were related in blood, language and religion to the Mycenaeans, but they showed little brotherly feeling for them. Everywhere they totally destroyed their cities. Many inhabitants were ruthlessly killed; others were made into slaves. A few – known as Ionian Greeks – escaped by fleeing from Greece altogether. They crossed the Aegean and settled along the coast of Asia Minor which became known as Ionia after them.

The Mycenaean civilization had come to an end. The whole Greek world was plunged into a Dark Age which lasted for 400 years, from 1200 to 800 B.C. It seemed that civilization had been lost and forgotten.

However, by 800 B.C., the long night was over. Again there had grown up cities at Athens, Thebes, Sparta, and throughout Greece. And there were also Greek cities now along the coast of Asia Minor where the Ionians had taken refuge.

Homer

Nor had the heritage of the past been completely destroyed. Some things of great value and importance survived the Dark Age. Throughout that time the bards must have gone on reciting their poems. During the Dark Age the art of writing had been lost. In about 800 B.C., however, the Greeks learned the use of the alphabet from the Phoenicians. Soon afterwards a blind bard called Homer put two of the traditional tales into writing.

One of these, the *Iliad*, is an account of a legendary episode which was supposed to have taken place towards the end of the Trojan War. It is in poetry and contains profound thought:

'My gallant lord, Tydeides,' the noble son of Hippolochus replied, 'what does my lineage matter to you? Men in their generations are like the leaves of the trees. The wind blows and one year's leaves are scattered on the ground; but the trees burst into bud and put on fresh ones when the spring comes round. In the same way one generation flourishes and another nears its end. But if you wish to hear about my family, I will tell you the tale . . .'

One of the earliest representations of Homer, on a Greek coin of the 4th century B.C.

The *Odyssey* describes the ten years' wandering of the Greek hero, Odysseus, on his way home from Troy, and is one of the most thrilling adventure stories ever told.

There was the time when Odysseus and his followers were trapped in the cave of a huge one-eyed giant called Polyphemus. After some of the Greeks had been eaten by this unpleasant character, Odysseus succeeded in blinding him by plunging a burning stake into his eye while he was asleep. Even so, it was not easy for the trapped men to escape, since Polyphemus kept a great stone at the mouth of the cave. Next morning, however, the giant removed this to take his sheep out to graze. The cunning and resourceful Odysseus at once seized the opportunity, tying his men to the underside of the sheep. The plan worked:

'Their master, though he was worn out by the agonies he had gone through, passed his hands along the backs of all the animals . . . but the idiot never noticed that my men were tied up under the breasts of his own woolly sheep.'

On another occasion Odysseus had the task of getting his ship past an island which was inhabited by bewitching water-sprites known as Sirens. No one, it was said, could resist their beautiful singing. But when they had enticed sailors into the shore, they promptly killed them:

There is no home-coming for the man who . . . hears the Sirens' voices; no welcome from his wife, no little children brightening at their father's return. For with the music of their song the Sirens cast their spell upon him, as they sit there in a meadow piled high with the mouldering skeletons of men, whose withered skin still hangs upon their bones.

To prevent any of his crew hearing the singing, Odysseus stopped up their ears with beeswax. But, like many another famous Greek, he was insatiably curious and could not bear to pass by without hearing the fabulous music. So he had his men bind his limbs and lash him tightly to the mast. In this way his curiosity could be gratified without endangering anyone:

'The lovely voices came to me across the water, and my heart was filled with such a longing to listen that with nod and frown I signed to my men to set me free. But they swung forward to their oars and rowed ahead, while Perimedes and Eurylochus jumped up, tightened my bonds and added more. However, when they had rowed past the Sirens and we could no longer hear their voices and the burden of their song, my good companions were quick to clear their ears of the wax I had used to stop them, and to free me from my shackles.'

Below: Odysseus, lashed to the mast of his ship, listens to the singing of the Sirens, represented as bird-like creatures. This comes from a Greek vase of the classical period.

Homer's books were the first writings in any European language, and so mark the beginning of European literature. No literature could have had a finer start.

The *Iliad* and the *Odyssey* were tremendously important to the Greeks. They were learned by generation after generation of schoolboys; while among adults a quotation from the *Iliad* would be used to support anything from a personal argument to a political treaty. Indeed, Homer's books are sometimes called 'the Bible of the Greeks', because they were almost as highly valued by them as the Old Testament stories were by the Hebrews. And, as with the Bible, the *Iliad* and the *Odyssey* taught the Greeks much about their religion.

Greek religion

Greek religion too had survived the Dark Age. The Greeks had twelve principal gods and goddesses, whom they thought of as being men and women just like themselves. But the gods were far more beautiful and powerful, and they did not die. Each god represented some aspect of nature. Their chief god was Zeus (later the Romans called him Jupiter), who was god of the sky. His wife was named Hera (Juno). Apollo was the god of the sun, and

Below left: Mount Olympus rises to about 9,570 feet. Its summit, where the Greek gods were said to live, is usually hidden by clouds.
Below: the war between the gods and the giants. On the right Zeus strikes with a thunderbolt; Athene is wielding her spear. This vase-painting, based on an ancient myth, shows just how human the Greeks believed their gods to be.

Athene, mourning. This relief of the goddess was carved between 470 and 450 B.C., and she is mourning for Athenians killed in the Persian Wars (see pages 131–3).

also of music and archery. Poseidon (Neptune) was god of the sea, and Ares (Mars) the god of war. Among the goddesses, apart from Hera, were Athene (Minerva), the goddess of wisdom, and Aphrodite (Venus), the goddess of love.

Homer tells how the twelve principal gods lived on the top of Mount Olympus, a high, usually cloud-capped mountain in the extreme north of Greece. But the Greeks also believed that the gods spent much of their time in the world of men – in Homer men were always meeting them. It was for this reason that the new cities contained so many temples. A temple was not a place where believers worshipped, but the actual home of the god and completely private to his use. Offerings were made outside; apart from priests, no one normally entered.

Although throughout Greece all gods were held in high esteem, each city had its own patron deity. Athens was so called because it was dedicated to the goddess Athene. The people built her a temple in the most sacred part of the city, sacrificed animals on her altar, and honoured her with regular festivals. In return, Athene protected the city and brought it victory in war.

In this respect, Athene may seem similar to the God of the Hebrews, but in other ways she was quite different. The Greek gods were stronger and cleverer than ordinary mortals, but they did not behave any better. Homer depicts them bickering with each other, lying, cheating, and frequently performing acts of disloyalty. Unlike Jehovah, such gods could hardly expect human beings to be perfect. So Greek religion did little to control people's conduct. The Olympians offered no rewards for righteousness. The idea of goodness pleasing God, and sin making him angry, has come to us from the Hebrews.

In addition to the twelve Olympians, there were countless other gods. Every aspect of nature, every hill, every river, every craft or profession had its own presiding spirit. The most important of these non-Olympian gods was Dionysus (Bacchus), the god of wine, who was later to become the patron deity of the theatre.

The unity of the Greeks

Greece never became a united country. The Greeks continued to live in small independent cities, as they had done in Mycenaean times. Furthermore, the relations between these cities were not always friendly; often they squabbled and made war on each other.

Yet, despite this, all Greeks were very aware that they belonged to the same race and shared the same civilization. The things

that bound them together were their common language, their common religion and their common love of Homer. And there was another thing which helped to bind them together, too. This was their common love of athletics.

The Olympic Games

With the Greeks, athletics were part of their religion. In the *Iliad*, when the friend of Achilles was killed, funeral games were held in his honour. Like epic poetry and religion, this practice of holding games survived through the Dark Age, so that in later times, regular athletic meetings took place all over Greece. One of these became more popular and important than the others. This was the meeting held every four years at Olympia, in southern Greece.

The first Olympic Games of which the Greeks kept a record took place in 776 B.C. It was not merely an athletics meeting, but a great religious festival dedicated to Zeus, the father of the gods.

When the time for the games drew near, three 'truce bearers of Zeus' went from Olympia throughout the Greek world. During the month of the festival, fighting had to cease everywhere, for a sacred peace was proclaimed.

Left: the 200 yards sprint.
Right, the 3-mile race.

Greek coin showing a racing chariot of the type used in the Olympic Games. Compare it with the Hittite chariot shown on page 99.

The games lasted only five days, although competitors had to arrive at Olympia at least a month before the commencement, so that they could do the last stages of their training under the eyes of the judges.

The first day was devoted to sacrifices and religious ceremonies. On the next day the chariot and horse races took place. Then came the foot races. There was a 200 yards sprint which was one length of the Olympic racing track, or stadium, so called because of the Greek word for this distance (see page 129). There was also a three-mile race.

Greek artists skilfully depict the different types of runners on their painted vases (compare illustrations above). The sprinters strain eagerly forward, running with pointed toes and violently swinging arms. The long-distance runners, on the other hand, run in a more relaxed way, on the balls of their feet, with erect bodies, and keeping their arms close to their sides.

These illustrations also show that the Greeks wore no clothes in their sports. They uncovered their bodies to the sun, with no feeling of false modesty, such as we might feel.

Other events included in the games were the long jump, throwing the discus (see illustration on page 139), hurling the javelin, boxing and wrestling. There were competitions for boys as well as for men, but women were not allowed to take part or even to watch. When all the contests had been decided, the great festival ended with a whole day devoted to feasting and rejoicing.

In the modern Olympic Games the winner receives a gold medal, but the prize awarded to a victorious athlete at a Greek Olympiad was nothing more than a wreath of wild olive leaves, which might be withered before he reached home. However, in the eyes of the Greeks, there was no greater honour that a young man could win than one of these simple Olympic crowns.

So important were the Olympic Games to the ancient Greeks that they reckoned their dates according to the Olympiads.

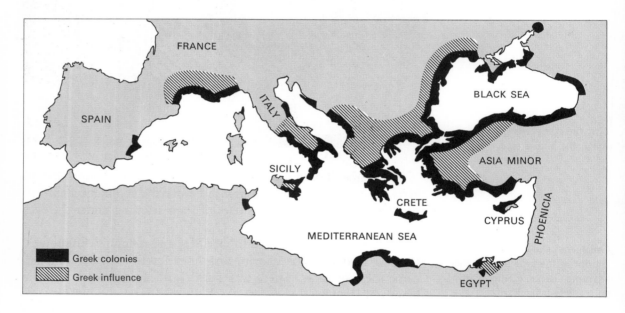

Greek colonies
Greek influence

The making of colonies

Above: Greek colonies and influence.

Between 750 and 600 B.C., countless Greek cities were founded along the coast of the Black Sea and the Mediterranean. It seems that at this time many more people were being born in Greece than that rather infertile country could support. So bands of adventurers sailed away from their native cities in search of somewhere to make a colony settlement. Thriving Greek colonies were established as far west as France and Spain.

However remote such places were from home each became, and remained, a true Greek city. Its citizens kept in touch with their mother-city, and were always conscious of the bond of loyalty and affection which tied them to their native land.

126

The olive harvest from a 6th-century Athenian vase. Two men beat the tree with sticks, while a boy has climbed it to knock down the topmost fruit. Olives are harvested like this today, except that nets are used to catch the falling fruit.

In the early days, Greek cities, both at home and abroad, depended for their livelihood on farming. But as time went on, some of them became important for their trade. Corinth was one of the great trading cities; and so was Athens, which sent its olive oil, its wine and its red and black pottery all over the Mediterranean world.

From the seventh century onwards, buying and selling was made much easier by the introduction of money. Coins were first minted in the kingdom of Lydia in Asia Minor, but it was not long before the Greek cities were striking their own. Like almost everything else the Greeks made, these were often very beautiful.

A terracotta (clay) model of a Greek trading vessel, probably a child's toy. Compare it with the Phoenician merchant ships on page 105.

The polis

Every Greek city, wherever it might be, was an independent city and an independent state: in fact, the Greeks used the same word to mean both 'state' and 'city'. The word was 'polis'. It is from this word that we get some of our own words dealing with cities and government. For instance, we call London, our principal city, the 'metropolis'. 'Politics' is the art of governing a state. The laws of a state are enforced by the 'police'.

A typical Greek *polis* included, in addition to the actual city, a large area of countryside where there were many farming villages. Thus the city-state of Athens included the territory known as Attica, and all Greeks living in Attica were Athenians, as much as the city-dwellers themselves.

The coming of democracy

Originally the city-states had been monarchies, each under the rule of a powerful king. Until the end of the Dark Age, the ordinary people counted for very little. They had no more rights and no more say in government than had the subject peoples of the first civilizations, or of the great oriental empires which followed them. In Greece, as in these eastern lands, there were city-dwellers, but no real citizens. However, from about 800 B.C., in many cities the situation changed.

The change took place in stages. First, the king was overthrown by the nobles. So monarchy came to an end and was replaced by a system of government known as oligarchy, in which families of noble blood or of great wealth had control of the state. Rule by one man had now given way to rule by 'the few'. But the ordinary people still had hardly any rights, and little influence on public affairs. Before they got them, the rule of 'the few' had to be replaced by the rule of 'the many'.

By 500 B.C., in a number of Greek cities this was happening: the ordinary people were struggling for political power and gaining the right to govern their own city-state.

The Greek word for 'people' was 'demos', so this system of government became known as 'democracy'.

Today, Britain and America, all the countries of the British Commonwealth and, indeed, most countries throughout the world, are democracies. That is why these developments which occurred 2,500 years ago in Greece are so important.

Yet although we call our own system of government a democracy, it is not a true system of democracy in the Greek sense. A modern state contains many millions of citizens, and this makes it

Greek coins were minted in a variety of designs. These four show:

1 Zeus on his throne.
2 A sea-horse.
3 An ear of wheat.
4 Athenian owl. 'Owls' were minted for several centuries and became the most widely used of all Greek coins. The letters on the right of the owl are the first three letters of Athens. The olive spray was not added until the early 5th century B.C. and may commemorate the Athenian victory at Marathon (see page 131).

1

2

3

4

impossible for everyone to have a direct say in policy-making. The idea of all British citizens attending parliamentary debates at Westminster is unthinkable. We vote for a member of Parliament, and rely on him to represent us, or speak on our behalf.

This is where the small Greek states had an advantage over large modern nations. Different states had different constitutions or, in other words, different sets of rules for organizing their government. But at Athens, when its democratic system had been perfected, every male citizen over the age of eighteen had the right to attend the Assembly in person.

The Assembly was their equivalent to our Parliament, and met about every ten days on a hill called the Pnyx. Only a small fraction of the 40,000 citizens would attend on any one occasion. All the same, it was a large gathering, and everyone had the right to express his views and to vote at the end of the debate. Thus it was the people themselves – acting directly, and not just through representatives – who decided what laws should be made, what taxes should be collected; and even, in times of crisis, whether there should be peace or war.

There is another way in which Greek democracy gave more power to the people than is possible in modern countries. At Athens the citizens not only made the laws; they performed all the duties of government. A Council of Five Hundred was chosen every year to watch over the day-to-day affairs of the city, control public expenditure, and prepare subjects for Assembly debates. Furthermore judges and magistrates were required to serve in the law courts, and there were many other state appointments.

All these positions were filled by ordinary people. So strongly did the Athenians believe that any citizen ought to be able to perform the duties that officers were not even elected by vote. They were chosen by lot – or 'out of the hat'.

This even applied to the highest position of all. Every day one member of the Council of Five Hundred was chosen to be Chairman – both of the Council and of the Assembly, if it was meeting. For twenty-four hours this person – however ordinary he might be – was head of the powerful state of Athens.

No wonder a citizen who might find himself in this position was interested in politics – he had to be! No wonder Athenians were proud when things went well for their city, and deeply concerned when events turned out badly. They themselves – not professional politicians – had taken all the decisions.

Nevertheless, if we are comparing Greek and British democracy, there are one or two things that have to be borne in mind on the other side. Not all Greek cities believed in giving power to the people. After Athens, the next most famous *polis* was Sparta. Here most citizens had little say in the running of affairs; for Sparta refused to move with the times, remaining an oligarchy in which the few had control of the state (see pages 30–31).

Moreover, even in democracies, women could not be citizens, and neither could foreigners or slaves. Slavery was an established institution in Greece, as it was throughout the ancient world. Athens had at least as many slaves as citizens. The majority of them were prisoners of war (or their descendants): unfortunate people from Egypt, Syria, Asia Minor, even from Greece itself, who had been captured in a campaign, and then brought to Athens by traders for sale in the market place.

Not all slaves were badly treated. Those who worked in the silver mines of Athens were; but many in domestic service had little to complain of; slaves who were well educated often held important jobs and became respected and wealthy. Still, whatever their jobs, they were the property of their masters, and could not do as they liked.

In Athens most citizens had one or more slaves. Greek democracy would hardly have been possible without them: how, without slaves, would there have been enough time to attend the Assembly?

Perhaps now this new political system does not seem so satisfactory as it did at first. But however uneasy we may be about slavery, the fact remains that it is in Greece that we find the first true citizens, and the first democracies, in which ordinary people count for something.

The new learning

At the same time as Greek citizens were getting into the habit of thinking for themselves about laws and taxes, they were beginning to think for themselves about other things also.

In ancient Sumer and Egypt priests and royal officials alone had been concerned with learning. But in the cities of Greece ordinary people had lively minds and were curious about a wide variety of subjects. Moreover, since the Phoenician alphabet had spread to Greece, ordinary people could easily learn how to read and write.

As a result of this increased mental activity, from the sixth century onwards, the Greeks gave the world a long line of philosophers or 'lovers of learning'. The earliest great philosopher was Thales who lived at Miletus, an Ionian city on the coast of Asia Minor.

In his young days Thales was a merchant and travelled to Egypt. Here he picked up many ideas which at that time were unknown in his own land. But the Greeks were not merely content to copy foreign ideas. They thought about and tried to develop what they learned. For instance, the Egyptians had a shadow clock which enabled them to tell the time by the sun.

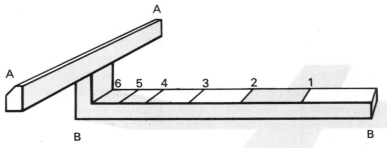

Egyptian shadow clock. In the morning the crosspiece (A–A) was turned towards the east, and as the sun rose in the sky, so the shadow thrown on the arm (B–B) shortened. At noon the clock was reversed, and the shadow cast by the descending sun gradually lengthened.

Thales – or it may have been his companion, Anaximander – realized that the same principle could be used to estimate the height of a pyramid.

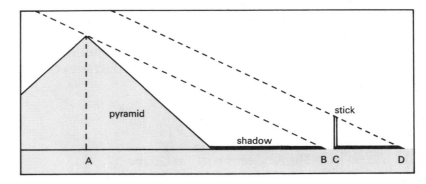

Right: measuring the height of a pyramid. The broken lines show the rays of the sun.

All that was necessary was to compare the length of the pyramid's shadow (A–B) with that of a stick (C–D). The stick could easily be measured. Then, if the shadow of the pyramid was a hundred times as long as the stick's shadow, the height of the pyramid must be a hundred times the stick's length.

Using the principle of the shadow clock in yet another way, Thales is said to have invented a method for estimating the distance of a ship out at sea. The diagram on the left shows how this is possible. If you measure the line AB along the shore and also measure the angle BAC, then the length of the line BC can be calculated by means of trigonometry or a scale drawing.

By such means Thales and his fellow philosophers became the

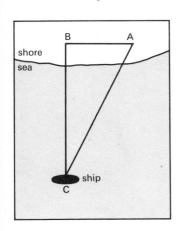

Below: measuring the distance of a ship out at sea.

first men to discover and understand some of the basic principles of geometry. And – what is more important – in developing ideas, stage by stage, in this way, they were using a kind of thinking which had hardly been practised before: reasoning.

The early Greek thinkers did not study only geometry; they were curious about everything. Thales's friend, Anaximander, interested himself in geography and is said to have made the earliest map of the world. This same philosopher also worked out a theory to explain how the human race came into being. The Greeks, like the Hebrews and other ancient peoples, had certain traditional stories about how men first entered the world. But Anaximander refused to accept these legendary explanations. Instead, he insisted on using his own mind to reason it out. He decided that man must have developed through lower forms of life, beginning with the fish. In other words, 2,500 years before Charles Darwin, Anaximander suggested what is now the generally accepted explanation of man's origin, the theory of evolution.

Even when Thales and his fellow philosophers arrived at wrong answers, they often asked questions – such as what the world was made of – which have interested men ever since. Certainly the world had known no thinkers of such daring and originality before.

But we have now reached the beginning of the fifth century B.C., which was the time when everything that the Greeks stood for was to be put to a severe test.

Dates to remember

about 2000 B.C. The Achaeans settle in Greece
         1400 B.C. Mycenaean civilization at its height
         1200 B.C. Dorian invasions
1200 to 800 B.C. Dark Age
about 800 B.C. Homer wrote the *Iliad* and the *Odyssey*
          776 B.C. First recorded Olympic Games
about 600 B.C. Thales living

Things to discuss

Would you prefer to live in a small state like Athens, or to be a citizen of a large country like Britain?

Things to do

1   The Mycenaean Greeks wrote in the so-called Linear B script, which was a development of the Minoan Linear A (see page

93). Find out something about Linear B, and how it differed from its predecessor.

2 Discover for yourself the story of the Trojan War described in Greek legend. What caused the war? How was Troy eventually captured?

3 Look up the name Heinrich Schliemann in one or two encyclopedias or reference books. What did he discover about the Mycenaean Greeks and the Trojans?

4 Write a few paragraphs describing the similarities and differences between the ancient and modern Olympic Games.

5 The Greeks are particularly famous for their wonderful legends. Try to read some of these during the next few weeks. Suitable books are suggested below.

Books to read

R. L. Green, *Tales of the Greek Heroes*, Puffin

R. L. Green, *Tales of Troy*, Puffin

E. K. Milliken, *The Greek People*, Harrap

C. E. Robinson, *Everyday Life in Ancient Greece*, Oxford University Press

M. and C. H. B. Quennell, *Everyday Things in Ancient Greece*, Batsford

The stadium at Delphi, where the Pythian Games were held in honour of Apollo. The stadium at Olympia was of turf only, but here there is a running track and tiers of stone seats. The 200 yards race started at the top end, and visitors can still see the parallel grooves in which, at the command 'Get ready!' the runners inserted their toes. The theatre shown on page 141 is near the stadium.

Chapter 8
Greek civilization at its height

In chapter 6 we read of the Persian empire which by 500 B.C. had gained control of the whole Middle East. This vast oriental state included Asia Minor. Not surprisingly, the little Ionian cities along the coast, like Miletus where Thales had lived, were compelled at first to pay tribute to the Persians.

But later they rose in revolt, and Athens, together with another mainland city, sent ships to help them. This infuriated Darius, the Persian emperor. When he had quelled the Greeks on the eastern side of the Aegean, he determined to attack Athens itself.

A great deal was at stake for the Greeks in their struggle with the Persians. The 'Great King' of Persia ruled by divine right and had complete power over the subject peoples of his empire.

But the Greeks had driven out their divine kings and developed a very different idea about how states should be governed. They believed in small free city-states, not in vast empires. Many of them believed also in democracy, that is, the rule of the people.

What would happen if the Persians were victorious? Would not democracy be at an end? And the first free citizens find themselves again at the mercy of an all-powerful king?

Fortunately, the Persians were not victorious. Greece was saved largely by the efforts of her two most famous cities.

Sparta

In the whole Greek world, no two cities were so unlike as Athens and Sparta. The Spartans were a strange people, quite different from the rest of their countrymen.

They believed themselves to be pure-blooded Dorians, and were very proud of this fact. When their ancestors had come down into Greece, they had treated the original inhabitants ruthlessly and made them into state serfs, tied to the land and compelled to grow food for the Spartans.

But it was not easy to keep these helots, as they were called, permanently enslaved, for they greatly outnumbered the Spartans. Once they had revolted and almost won control; the Spartans were determined that this should never happen again. So they concentrated solely on the defence of the state. Every year they made a formal declaration of war on the helots. The city became a permanent armed camp. Only citizens who could fight were any use to the Spartans; babies that were weak or had any physical defects were callously taken out on to a mountainside and left to die.

On reaching seven, boys and girls had to leave their parents and join regular training companies composed of children of the same age. Their upbringing was extremely tough. They were expected to endure heat and cold, hunger and thirst, physical pain and harsh punishments. To teach them cunning, they were encouraged to steal; but if caught, they got a severe beating – not for their crime, but for their carelessness. Periodically, too, they were encouraged to go out and murder a few helots.

Such atrocities were as horrible as anything that could be found in the Persian empire. Yet, we have to realize also that the Spartans became the toughest, best disciplined and bravest soldiers in the whole ancient world. And these qualities – although they were paid for at an appalling price – did much at this hour of crisis to save Greece.

A girl running, thought to be a Spartan. Unlike Athenian girls, Spartan girls were given the same athletic training as boys. This bronze statuette dates from about the same time as the Persian Wars.

The Persian Wars

But the Athenians also proved tough and courageous. Indeed, the Athenians had to bear the brunt of the first Persian attack almost alone. When, in 490 B.C., a large enemy army landed at Marathon, within a few miles of their city, they immediately sent to Sparta for help. But owing to a religious festival the Spartans delayed their departure several days and by the time they arrived the battle was over. Aided only by a small force from one other city, the freeman army of Athens had totally routed the Persians. When the Spartans arrived, all they saw were the 6,400 dead the Persians had left behind on the field.

However, ten years later, under their new emperor Xerxes, the Persians again invaded Greece, this time with an army of truly fantastic size. To get his men across from Asia Minor to Europe, Xerxes built a bridge of boats at the Dardanelles. Then his huge army moved by the coastal road down into Greece, with a supporting fleet a mile or so out at sea, keeping alongside.

Now it was the turn of the Spartans to show their mettle. This they did by their heroic defence of the pass at Thermopylae (480 B.C.). For days the Spartan king Leonidas, with a tiny body of Spartans and other troops, defied the whole might of the Persians. Nor were they allowed to pass until the last of the three

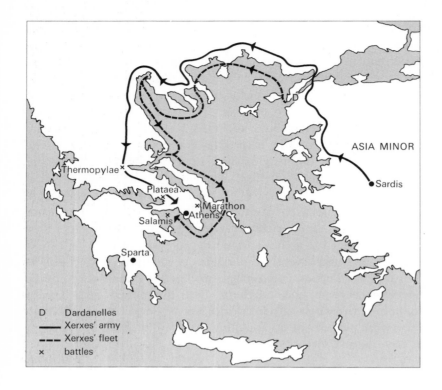

Left: the Persian Wars.

hundred brave Spartans had been killed: The memorial column erected at Thermopylae in their honour had these words carved upon it:

> Go, tell the Spartans, thou that passest by,
> That here obedient to their laws we lie.

But now the road was open to Athens. When Xerxes arrived, he found that its citizens had evacuated their women and children, and largely abandoned the city. Yet this was with no intention of giving in to the enemy. Rather, the Assembly had wisely decided that the only chance they had of defeating the Persians was by fighting them at sea. From their ships, the citizens watched the sky turn red as the Persians set fire to their homes and their temples.

But they avenged themselves soon afterwards by heavily defeating the Persian fleet in a battle at Salamis. This setback destroyed the morale of the Persians and caused Xerxes to hurry half his army back across the Dardanelles. True, he left orders that the rest should complete the conquest of Greece. However, this was not an easy task, for the morale of the Greeks was very high. Again under the leadership of the Spartans, they finally

Greek soldiers fighting.
A two-edged sword carried
in a scabbard at the waist,
and a long spear held in the
right hand are their weapons.
For armour they wear bronze
helmets and corselets and,
protecting their legs below
the knee, bronze greaves.

defeated the Persian army at the battle of Plataea. And the impossible had happened: Greece had been saved.

The classical Greeks

In many ways during the period which followed, the free cities of Greece behaved unreasonably. The Athenians were convinced that the Persian armies would return a third time. They were also convinced that the only way to stop them was for the Greek cities to become united under their own leadership. Many of them did so, contributing money and helping to keep a combined fleet in being. But Athens became somewhat high-handed and began to treat the other states as her subjects, rather than as equal allies; what had originally been a league of free cities developed into the Athenian empire.

Meanwhile Sparta grew alarmed at Athenian power and organized a rival league under her own leadership. Eventually this led to the Peloponnesian War (431–404 B.C.) which involved most Greek cities both at home and abroad, and ended in the victory of Sparta over Athens. Nor was this all. Bickering and inter-state warfare continued until – 140 years after the defeat of

Persia – a new conqueror, Philip of Macedon, arrived on the scene. So exhausted and demoralized were the once proud Greek cities by this time that there was nothing they could do but to submit to him.

Yet, despite these blunders and disasters, the period between the defeat of Xerxes in 479, and the coming of the Macedonians in 338, was the most brilliant period in Greek history. It was probably the most brilliant period in the whole history of western man. This is one of the reasons we refer to the 5th and 4th centuries B.C. as the 'classical' period, and speak of the Greeks who lived at this time as the 'classical Greeks'.

The greatest of all Greek cities during the classical period was undoubtedly the democratic state of Athens.

In democracy it is the people themselves who have the real power. But if they are to act wisely they still need good leadership. The finest achievements of democracy usually come when the people find a great statesman to lead them.

The age of Pericles

Soon after the Persian Wars the Athenians found such a leader. His name was Pericles and he was in control of affairs from 460 to 430 B.C. Pericles was a man of bold imagination, and a fine speaker. His ambition was to make Athens 'the school of Greece', in other words, an example to all the Greeks.

One of the things the Athenians did under his leadership was to rebuild their temples on the Acropolis, which had been destroyed by the Persians.

Every Greek city had its acropolis, or 'upper city'. At Athens this was a flat-topped rock, less than a quarter of a mile long, which rose about 150 feet above the surrounding plain. From the earliest times it had been the most sacred place. Now, under Pericles, the citizens determined to make it the most impressive and beautiful place also. In this they succeeded. All the buildings inside the walled enclosure were of marble, and were designed in what we know as the 'classical style' of architecture.

Classical architecture

It is worth learning a little about this 'classical style', for it is to be found in many of the churches, town halls and other public buildings of our own country. Its most striking feature is the use of columns. The stone column had been invented in Egypt, but it was the Greeks who perfected it. Eventually they had three 'orders', or types of column: the Doric, the Ionic and the

Pericles. This marble bust is a copy of Roman date from the Greek original that had been made in Pericles' lifetime, and can be seen today in the British Museum.

The Acropolis. From the lower
entrance (A), which is of Roman
date, the visitor climbs past the
Temple of Victory (B) to the
original monumental entrance
gateway (C). In ancient times the
colossal bronze statue of Athene
stood at (D), with the Erechtheum
(E) and the Parthenon (F) beyond.
The Theatre of Dionysus is
marked (G); the other theatre-
like building (H) is Roman.
Note the Acropolis wall (I).

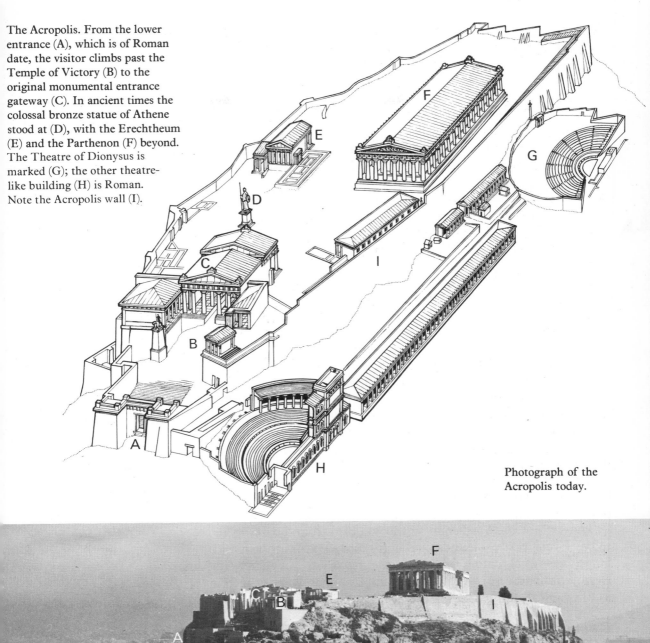

Photograph of the
Acropolis today.

The 'classical orders'.
The Doric (*left*), which
originated on the mainland of
Greece, is the simplest and
oldest (from 7th century
B.C.). The Ionic (*centre*) was
the next to be developed: as its
name implies, in the eastern
Aegean. It can easily be
recognized by the scroll design
of the capital. The Corinthian
(*right*) dates from the 5th
century B.C. Here the capital is
deeper and more elaborate,
carved with acanthus foliage.

Corinthian (see above). In any large town you could easily find examples of all three styles.

On the Acropolis, the monumental entrance gateway was built in the Ionic style; so, too, was the graceful little Temple of Victory. But the noblest building of all, the Parthenon, is in the Doric style.

The Parthenon (Temple of the Maiden) was the shrine of Athene, the patron goddess of Athens. Like all classical architecture, it was extremely simple in design. It was oblong, with a double row of columns at each end, and a single row down each side. The whole was covered by a low-pitched roof, in such a way as to form a gable, or pediment, at the front and back of the building. These pediments were filled with magnificent statues of the gods; while, high on the walls inside the colonnade, a band of carved marble depicted the people of Athens moving in stately procession on the occasion of Athene's own festival.

The shell of the Parthenon still looks down from the Acropolis today. Every year thousands of people from all parts of the world go to see it. No other building can match its simplicity, its elegant proportions, its quiet perfection. It has been described as 'the most thrilling building there is'.

Classical sculpture

The stone carvings which decorated the Parthenon were the work of the Athenian sculptor, Pheidias. He also made two statues of the goddess Athene. One, which was covered in ivory and gold, was kept in the temple itself. The other was of bronze and stood out on the open Acropolis. It was over 70 feet high. Such was the civic pride of the Athenians and their reverence for the goddess

Above: the Parthenon. Finished in 432 B.C., it remained a temple of Athene for nine centuries. From about A.D. 450 to 1458, it served as a Christian church, but then Athens was taken by the Turks and the Parthenon was converted into a Mohammedan mosque. In 1687, when Venetians were attacking the city, one of their shells fell on it and ignited a Turkish powder store inside. But for this mishap, the Parthenon would probably still be a complete building.

Part of the west frieze of the Parthenon, showing horsemen, with attendants, preparing to take part in a procession.

141

who – so they believed – had delivered them from the Persians.

The statues of Athene have been lost, but much of the sculpture from the frieze and pediments of the Parthenon was brought to Britain in the 19th century by Lord Elgin. These 'Elgin Marbles', as they are called, can now be seen in the British Museum.

The Greek sculptors did not only work on religious subjects. They made superb statues of the human figure, and delighted to immortalize in bronze or stone the great Olympic winners. In a statue like the *Discus Thrower* (opposite), the controlled, uncoiling power of the athlete is magnificently portrayed.

Perhaps no people have been so much concerned with beauty as the classical Greeks. Athenian citizens lived in very plain court-yard houses. But in their rooms were beautiful drinking cups and water jugs, lovely mirrors and jewellery, and pretty dolls for the children. Even Greek coins of the period are little masterpieces.

Above: clay doll with movable arms and legs which may have belonged to a Corinthian child in the 4th century B.C. How does it compare with the Egyptian tomb figures in chapter 4?

Marble statue of a man carrying a calf, made in the mid 6th century B.C., at least a hundred years before the *Discus Thrower*. The pose is stiff and formal, reminding us of Egyptian art, from which the early Greek sculptors learned a great deal. Artists like Pheidias and Myron broke away from the ancient tradition and succeeded in making completely lifelike figures. But today many people prefer the simplicity of 6th-century sculpture. What do you think?

Right: horse's head from the east pediment of the Parthenon. At one end of the pediment Helios, the Sun god, drives his chariot up out of the sea as day breaks. At the other end the Moon goddess, Selene, sinks below the horizon in her four-horse chariot. This is one of her horses. Pheidias portrays its tiredness after its long journey across the heavens.

The *Discus Thrower* by Myron. This is an early copy, the original bronze having been lost. Myron and Pheidias worked in Athens at about the same time.

The invention of drama

Though the Athenians produced some of the finest architecture and sculpture, the basic ideas came from elsewhere. But one art they developed on their own. This was the art of drama, as practised ever since throughout the western world.

Europe's first theatre stands immediately below the Parthenon. Long before the theatre itself was built, an annual festival dedicated to Dionysus, the god of wine and fruitfulness, had been held at the same spot. This ancient ceremony was performed by choruses of men, clad in goat-skins, who sang and danced in the god's honour. Spectators gathered in a ring to watch the dancers, and presently this led to the marking out of a permanent circle (see figure 1, right). Later still, tiers of seats were erected round half of it (figure 2). This, by the way, is the reason the lower gallery in our own theatres is known as 'the circle'. The Greeks called the level ground in the centre, where the performance took place, the orchestra, which is another term we have inherited from them.

At first the performers only sang and danced, but then the Athenians began to experiment with actors who spoke and 'played' their parts, between the sung choruses. On the side of the orchestra opposite the public seats, a tent or booth was erected for the performers. When actors were introduced, this was made into the stage (figure 3).

Even in the time of Pericles an Athenian could only go to the theatre during the Festival of Dionysus. But at the Festival there was a feast of drama. Three poets were chosen every year, and each wrote a series of three tragedies based on some well-known Greek legend. For example, the playwright Aeschylus dramatized the legend of Prometheus, whom the Greeks said had given fire to mankind by stealing it from heaven. As a punishment Zeus ordered him to be chained to a mountainside, where an eagle fed every day on his liver, and the amount that the eagle devoured grew again during the night. But Prometheus endured his torments and, far from asking for mercy, continued to hurl defiance at Zeus, the King of the Gods.

These plays were written in poetry which stirred the emotions of the audience deeply. They gave the Athenians much to think about, too, for they dealt with the eternal problems of human life and human conduct, and with the proper relationship between men and the gods. People have been thinking about the tragedies of Aeschylus, Sophocles and Euripides ever since.

In an altogether lighter vein, there were other plays known as

Development of the theatre.

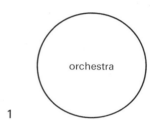

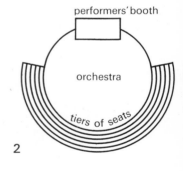

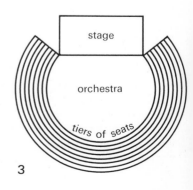

Theatre of Dionysus at Delphi today. People are watching a performance of a tragedy by Sophocles. The orchestra is used by the chorus, which always plays a major part in Greek tragedies. Theatres of this type were eventually introduced into Britain by the Romans: the one at St Albans, Hertfordshire, is illustrated on page 186.

comedies. These were full of ready wit and jokes about topical events, often poking fun at the leading politicians and citizens of the day. The greatest writer of comedies was Aristophanes, whose plays are still frequently performed.

The citizens of Athens took a tremendous interest in their theatre. An average audience would number 10,000, while over 1,000 men and boys performed in the plays each year. Then, too, the festival was run as a public competition; and it was a jury of ordinary citizens who had the job of judging the plays and awarding the prizes: one for the best comedy and another for the best series of tragedies.

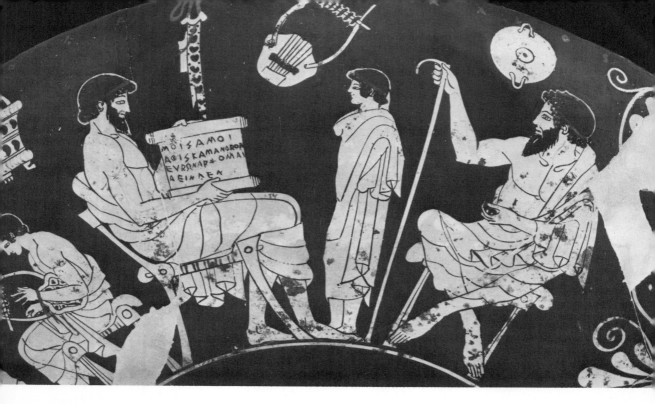

Classical learning

Most Athenians were not highly educated in our sense. Girls did not go to school at all; they were merely taught housecraft by their mothers. Boys attended private schools, which were usually run by poor or elderly citizens. Here they studied reading, writing and arithmetic, and learned a great deal of poetry by heart, particularly the poetry of Homer. They were also taught to sing and to play the lyre, since music, like poetry, was considered very important in the training of character.

Very important, too, were gymnastics, for the proper training of the body. The state itself looked after this part of education, by providing public baths and gymnasia where boys could learn to swim, ride, and practise athletics. Most boys left school at sixteen, but the sons of rich parents were able to continue their education by attending classes given by advanced teachers known as sophists. With a sophist, young men could study oratory (the art of speaking persuasively), mathematics, astronomy, history, literature, philosophy, and many other subjects.

For anyone curious about the world, and man's place in it, growing up in the Athens of Pericles must have been an exhilarating experience. The city seethed with new ideas affecting every

An Athenian school. The boy in the centre is reciting Homer's *Iliad* from a scroll held by the master. The man seated on the right is the pedagogue – a family slave who brought the boy to school, stayed with him during his lessons and, as the cane in his hand suggests, kept a strict eye on his behaviour at all times.

branch of learning; challenging and important discoveries were being made on every side. One teacher named Anaxagoras suddenly shocked Athenians by announcing that the moon did not shine with its own light, but merely reflected the light of the sun. Today we know that Anaxagoras was right, though hardly anyone would believe him at the time.

The advances which the classical Greeks made in knowledge depended on three things. The first we have already discussed in talking about Thales and Anaximander (see page 128). Instead of blindly accepting what religion and legend said about the world, the Greeks insisted on using their own minds to think and reason.

To appreciate the difference this made, let us take the example of medicine. The old superstitious belief was that diseases were caused by evil demons, and that the only hope of curing a sick person was by means of rituals and charms. Even the writings of the Egyptians, from which the Greeks learned much, were full of magical recipes and incantations. But progressive Greek doctors would have nothing to do with such methods. They were convinced that diseases had natural, not supernatural, causes. And they believed that these natural causes could be discovered by the use of reasoned thought. This is now the modern view. It is not a demon but a virus that causes measles.

The second thing the classical thinkers did was to look carefully at the natural world and gather together all the facts they could about it. Again, if we take the doctors as our example, this meant that they had to study carefully the organs of the human body, as well as observe and note down the symptoms of various diseases. By such means, they were able to build up a collection of reliable information to help them in their later work.

A Greek doctor examining a patient. The figure looking on, with a snake coiled round his staff, may be Aesculapius, the Greek god of medicine.

The third thing the classical thinkers did was to experiment. Thus the doctors experimented with various ways of curing illnesses, until, by trial and error, they hit upon the best treatment.

The Greeks were the first men really to develop and combine these three ways of obtaining knowledge. All our own scientific discoveries depend on the same three principles: 1 the use of reason, 2 the collection of facts, and 3 experiment. Thus it is perfectly true to say that the Greeks invented science; though we must not forget the great debt which they owed to earlier peoples.

Herodotus tried to apply the same scientific principles in writing the first history book, which has earned him the title 'the father of history'.

Before Herodotus there was no history; only legends. These legends often contained a grain of truth, but there was also a mountain of fiction. Fantastic stories about the heroes and the gods were all very well, but Herodotus wanted to discover what had actually happened in history and why it had happened.

His book was a history of the whole ancient world, but particularly of the Persian Wars. To find out about the ancient world, he questioned travellers who had seen historic monuments in far-off lands. To find out about the Persian Wars, he listened to the tales of old soldiers who had fought in them. In this way he collected all the facts he could. He also made long journeys to gather additional information, and test the truth of what he heard.

Still, there remained a good deal of legend and hearsay in the history of Herodotus, and it was left to another famous Greek historian, Thucydides, to perfect the scientific method of studying the subject. He wrote a detailed account of the Peloponnesian War, in which he himself had served as a general. We can tell how anxious Thucydides was to discover the truth and find out exactly what happened from the following quotation:

With regard to my factual reporting of the events of the war I have made it a principle not to write down the first story that came my way, and not even to be guided by my own general impressions; either I was present myself at the events which I have described or else I heard of them from eye-witnesses whose reports I have checked with as much thoroughness as possible.

We have spoken in detail only of medicine and history. But the same scientific approach to knowledge was extended to every field of inquiry. Using the new methods, Aristotle, who lived some

Scientific collection of facts. This section of a papyrus on astronomy is covered with explanatory diagrams. It is written in Greek and comes from Egypt where many Greek ideas spread (see pages 153–5).

Right: Socrates. He has been called not only one of the wisest but also one of the ugliest men in history. However, he was enormously tough and strong. On campaign as an infantryman during the Peloponnesian War, he remained cheerful in the harshest winter conditions, and in battle set others an example by his courage.

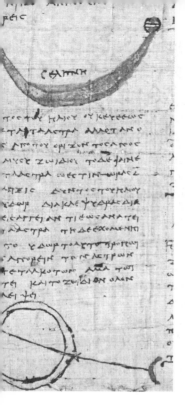

time after Pericles, from 384 to 322 B.C., studied physics, botany, biology, politics, literature, and many other subjects. Nothing could satisfy his appetite for facts. In his books Aristotle left a greater collection of information on all kinds of subjects than had ever been brought together before.

Aristotle was also a renowned teacher, and founded a school at Athens called the Lyceum. This, together with the school Plato founded, known as the Academy, marks in effect the beginning of the European university system.

Socrates

Most Greek men of learning were writers, like Herodotus, Thucydides and Aristotle. Yet the greatest of all Athenian thinkers built up his reputation simply on a lifetime of talk. This man was Socrates, of whom it is said that he never wrote a word.

The Athenians were great talkers. Debates, conversations and arguments were going on all the time: in the Assembly, in the market place, in the gymnasia, and in the homes of citizens. Nothing helped so much to educate the Athenians as this never-ending flow of talk.

But Socrates would out-talk any man. With him, furthermore, it was never idle chit-chat. He had a way of turning every conversation into a serious search after truth. People had to think carefully when they spoke to Socrates, for if they said anything foolish he would soon point out the mistake in their argument.

Socrates was not much interested in science or even in history. His main concern was with moral and spiritual matters. He tried to find out what goodness was. He decided that goodness was wisdom, and that the sole cause of wrong-doing was ignorance. So he did his best to make the young who came to him more thoughtful, in the hope that they would become wiser and better citizens. In fact he believed that he had a mission to make people think. Socrates practised what he preached, as this story written by his pupil Plato shows:

One day about dawn a thought struck him, and he stood still, thinking about it; and when he made no progress, he did not give it up; he went on standing and searching. Midday came, and people began to notice, and said to each other 'Socrates has been standing there thinking since early morning!' In the end some of the Ionians, in the evening after dinner . . . brought their palliasses out, to sleep in the fresh air, and incidentally to watch Socrates and see if he would stand all night too; and he did, until dawn came again and the sun rose; and then he said a prayer to the sun-god and went his way.

With his deep concern for truth, Socrates was forever challenging accepted beliefs and upsetting other people's smug convictions. He even cast doubts on the sacred stories in Homer, and was rumoured to have said, 'Of the gods we know nothing.' Eventually, at the age of nearly seventy, he was charged with not believing in the city's gods and corrupting the minds of the young. But Socrates had his own god: a higher, finer spirit than that of the twelve Olympians. 'O Athenians,' he proclaimed at his trial, 'I love and honour you, but I will obey god rather than you.'

By a narrow majority, a jury of his fellow citizens found him guilty, and he was condemned to death. Even so he could have escaped. One of his friends bribed the jailer, but Socrates refused to go:

Shall I not obey the laws that have protected me until now? I stood my ground in the army, where my generals posted me; shall I not stay at my post now, where god has placed me?

When the appointed day came, after a long discussion on what would happen to his soul at death, he calmly drank the official cup of poison. In so doing, he kept faith with what was perhaps his noblest principle: that 'it is better to suffer injustice than to do it'.

His follower Plato could never forgive the Athenians for putting Socrates to death. Partly because of this, and also because he felt that the ordinary citizen was incapable of true wisdom, Plato became a severe critic of Greek democracy. The man in the street, he declared, was not fit to control the affairs of the city. Good government would come only when it was left to the lovers of wisdom or philosophers.

Perhaps there was more than a grain of truth in Plato's argument. Thucydides, who had lived through the follies and horrors of the Peloponnesian War, also questioned whether democracy was the best form of government. In normal circumstances, Athenian citizens could be relied upon to vote for reasonable policies, but in times of tension, when the atmosphere of the Assembly became charged with passion, they sometimes refused to listen to moderate opinions and were carried away by ambitious and militaristic men. In the end, their failure to act sensibly led to the decline of the city-state and ultimately to the Macedonian take-over of all Greece.

Yet no other ancient people have made so many inventions and discoveries of importance, or cast such a spell over the future.

Part of a vase-painting showing a vase-painter at work. In the 6th century B.C. figures were painted in black on the yellow, orange or red of the clay background (e.g. the vase opposite). In the 5th century Athenian painters began 'blacking in' the background, and leaving the figures in the natural clay (as above). Look through this and the previous chapter to see which are the earlier and which the later vases.

Right: Ajax and Achilles playing a board-game. This is a fine example of the vase-painter's art. Greek vases were produced in large numbers, so there may be some in your local museum. They depict every aspect of Greek life.

151

What was their secret? It was their love of political and personal freedom. For everything else they achieved depended on it.

If we wish to confirm this, we need only compare Athens with the entirely different city-state of Sparta. Nowhere, men said, were people more obedient to authority than in Sparta. Every citizen was compelled to become a soldier, and all the ordinary pleasures of life were forbidden: so much so, that we still speak of a life of extreme plainness and discipline as 'a Spartan existence'.

The Spartans were loyal citizens, courageous men and good fighters. But they produced no poets, or scientists, or philosophers. There were no impressive buildings either; and no art, no drama, no sculpture. It is true that at one moment of crisis the Spartans helped to save Greece. But apart from this, what do we owe to Sparta?

The answer must be 'very little', but where should we be today without reasoned thought, science, democratic citizenship, and all the other things we have inherited from the Athenians and the freedom-loving Greeks?

Dates to remember

490 B.C.   The battle of Marathon
480 B.C.   Xerxes invades Greece
460–430 B.C.   The age of Pericles

Things to discuss

Without slavery the wonderful achievements of ancient Athens would probably have been impossible. Yet some Athenians in the age of Pericles wanted all slaves to be set free. Pretend you are an Athenian citizen and discuss whether the city should abolish slavery or not.

Things to do

1   Look through chapters 7 and 8, and make a list of all the English words that are of Greek origin. By using a dictionary which gives the origins of words, discover some more for yourself. (For instance, in the *Concise Oxford Dictionary* under the word 'tragedy' you will find it says 'f. Gk. *tragoidia*'. The list of abbreviations at the front tells you that f. = from, and Gk. = Greek. So 'f. Gk. *tragoidia*' means 'from the Greek word tragoidia'.)

2 Find out more about the upbringing of boys and girls in Sparta and Athens. Say what you think were the strengths and weaknesses of each type of education.

3 Find out more about the city of Athens in the age of Pericles, then describe an imaginary visit there.

4 See if you can discover examples of the three orders of classical column in your own district. Make drawings of what you find.

Books to read
D. R. Barker, *The Story of Ancient Athens*, E. Arnold
D. Taylor, *Ancient Greece*, Methuen

Young men playing hockey, from a marble relief of the 6th century B.C.

Chapter 9
The spread of Greek civilization

The creative period of the early civilizations was followed by a period of great conquests and great empires. Now, after the classical Greek civilization, it is conquests and empires that dominate our story again. First came the Macedonian empire of Alexander the Great, and second the Roman empire.

In both cases the making of these empires meant the defeat of the Greek people. But in both cases also, in the words of the Roman poet Horace: 'Captive Greece made captive her rude conqueror.' In other words, the Macedonians and the Romans took over the classical Greek civilization. Then, as the two empires expanded – the first to the east, the second to the west – so the Greek ideas, which they had accepted, were carried into ever wider areas of the world.

The Macedonians

In the extreme north of the Greek peninsula lay Macedonia, a country which was inhabited by a people of the same origin as the Greeks. Macedonia was a barren and mountainous land and, for the most part, its inhabitants were shepherds or simple farmers, knowing nothing of city life. They were certainly far less civilized than the Greeks, who had always regarded them as barbarians.

We have seen before, however, that a backward people can easily overcome a more advanced race. Indeed, one of the lessons of ancient history is that this is almost bound to happen whenever the civilized are at loggerheads among themselves, or show signs of weakness and exhaustion. Because of the Peloponnesian War and the bitterness and strife which followed it (see page 133), this was now the case with the Greeks.

Even so, when we remember how heroically they had resisted the Persians, it hardly seems possible that, only 140 years later, this same people would be willing to surrender to the Macedonians: and that with scarcely so much as a struggle.

It is true that many Greek cities thought they had good reason for their unheroic conduct. Philip, the king of Macedonia, claimed that he was no enemy of the Greeks. He had already adopted their language as the language of his own court, and was having his son educated in Greek ways by the Athenian-trained philosopher Aristotle. Furthermore, the Macedonians had no intention of actually conquering Greece. The only thing Philip demanded was the formation of a league of Greek cities under his leadership. In this way, he hoped to bring unity at last to their divided land; and he even promised to lead them in a war against their old enemies the Persians. Philip claimed that he was coming, not as a conqueror, but as a friend and champion of the Greeks.

Many city-states, in their weakness and exhaustion, were prepared to believe him. Yet all thinking Greeks knew that the moment they submitted to Philip, the complete independence which they had once valued so highly would be at an end.

However, in 338 B.C., submit to Philip they did. Only Athens, with a few other Greek cities, sent soldiers to resist the Macedonians; and after they had been defeated in a single battle, only the indomitable Spartans refused to join the League of Corinth which Philip then formed.

Alexander the Great

But in 336 B.C. Philip was suddenly murdered by a fellow Macedonian, and was succeeded by his twenty-year-old son Alexander. Some of the Greeks, hoping that this young man would be easier to deal with than his father, at once rose in revolt. But their hopes were unfounded. Alexander put down the rebellion with greater determination and ruthlessness than even Philip had shown. As an example of what would happen if there were any further trouble, the city of Thebes was razed to the ground, and its inhabitants sold into slavery.

With the Greeks again cowed into submission, Alexander turned his attention to the invasion of Persia, which had already been planned by his father. He declared that his purpose was to take revenge on the Persians for their invasion of Greece; and also that he wished to spread Greek ideas into the continent of Asia. But it seems likely that there was a further reason, about which he was less outspoken. This was his own burning ambition and love of power.

Alexander spent the next dozen years entirely in fighting and wars of conquest. In a series of brilliant campaigns, he captured Asia Minor, Syria, Palestine and Egypt, eventually overcoming the Persian king and taking over his empire altogether.

Alexander had now 'avenged Greece', but he was still not satisfied. He marched his army eastward, through Afghanistan, into India – until he was at last stopped by his own soldiers who refused to go any farther.

Portrait of Alexander on a coin dated 326 B.C.

155

The 'greatness' of Alexander, the 'glamour' of his deeds, and the fascination of his character impressed his contemporaries. Many modern historians, too, admire Alexander. They claim that he was an explorer as well as a soldier; and indeed, he took with him on his marches, not only official historians, but scientists to collect information for Aristotle. It is also argued that Alexander's ambition was to harmonize all the races he conquered into one state; that he had a vision of the 'brotherhood of man', and of 'one world' – naturally with Alexander himself as king.

But whatever ideals he may have had, this much is certain: that his actual career was one of ruthless brutality and countless ugly deeds. And, like other conquerors, as victory followed victory, he became more intoxicated by his own greatness; until in the end, his subjects were expected to bow down before Alexander and acknowledge him as a god.

We must bear in mind that he lived in an age when brutality in war was commonplace; and when gods were thought of as being like superhuman men, and therefore superhuman men could easily imagine themselves to be gods. But after making such allowances, it seems doubtful whether a man who caused so much bloodshed and sought power to the extent that Alexander

Alexander's exploits appealed to men's imagination through the ages. This French miniature of A.D. 1463 shows his invasion of the Punjab (Indus Valley), where the king, Poros, tried to defeat him, using 200 trained elephants to terrify his men. But Alexander outmanoeuvred him and Poros (*centre background*) surrendered. After the battle, Alexander's troops refused to go any farther.

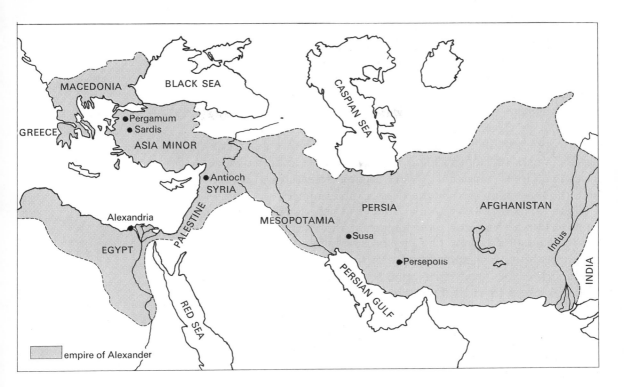

Empire of Alexander the Great.

did deserves our unqualified admiration. He was not, as one modern writer has called him, 'the most wonderful man who ever lived'.

Alexander died suddenly in 323 B.C. at the age of thirty-two, leaving no heir and no plan for the government of his empire. After years of tumult and confusion, three large new kingdoms eventually emerged, based on Egypt, Mesopotamia and Macedonia. Each was ruled by one of Alexander's old generals who, like their master, came to think of themselves as divine kings.

The spread of Greek ideas

Although Alexander and the men who followed him copied Persian ideas of government and divine kingship, they tried in many other ways to spread the ideas of Greek civilization.

Throughout the territories which the Macedonians conquered, new cities were founded which were run on Greek lines. Such cities were left to manage their own local affairs through a democratic assembly of citizens. Their powers could not compare with those of the classical Athenians: they had to pay tribute to the king, and were generally watched over by a royal garrison. Nevertheless, a little of the Greek tradition of citizenship and democracy was allowed to survive.

The new cities were modelled in other ways on those of Greece. Each had fine public buildings designed in the classical style; each had its gymnasium, where young men practised Greek athletics; each had its theatre, where thousands of citizens would sit under the open skies watching Greek plays. In every city the Greek language was spoken, at least by the upper classes, who also wrote in Greek. Then there were great libraries of books, which contained the masterpieces of Greek literature and learning: the works of Homer, Plato, Aristotle and Herodotus. Some places had Greek 'museums', where original research was carried on in the subjects studied by the classical philosophers.

There were many such cities, like Antioch, Sardis and Pergamum. But perhaps the most important was Alexandria, which was the capital of Egypt. This city became fabulously wealthy on the profits of its wide-spread trade. Particularly valuable were the rare and precious goods that came from the east, by way of the Red Sea. It was through the markets of Alexandria (and its rival, Antioch, in Syria) that luxuries like silk, pepper and spices reached the west for the first time. Because they had travelled over long distances they were very costly.

In appearance, Alexandria was a city of great magnificence. Its large and busy harbour was dominated by a gigantic lighthouse, the beacon of which could be seen far out to sea at night. Beyond the harbour was the palace of the Macedonian kings of Egypt, surrounded by spacious gardens. Here, also, were the marble buildings of the Royal Museum, with its exhibition rooms, lecture halls, laboratories, dissecting rooms, observatory, and its splendid library containing 100,000 books.

Because of the unrivalled facilities which Alexandria offered for research and study, the best brains in the world were attracted to it. Eventually, it outstripped even Athens as the foremost centre of classical learning.

Above: lighthouse of Alexandria, from a Roman coin of the 2nd century A.D.

Papyrus letter from Alexandria of the 1st century A.D. The writer asks to be sent drugs of good quality. (The letter is in the British Museum.)

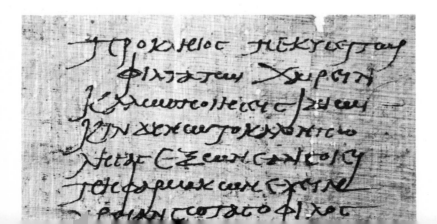

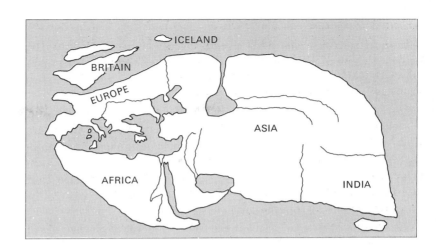

Map of the world according to Eratosthenes.

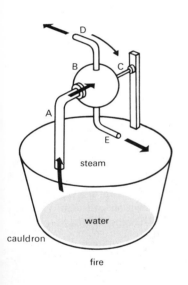

Hero's steam turbine. The cauldron of water was heated to boiling point by the fire beneath. Steam rushed up the tube (A) into the hollow ball (B), which was pivoted on the rod (C). The only way the steam could escape was through the bent tubes (D, E), and the thrust of this escaping steam sent the ball spinning round in the opposite direction.

Alexandria was particularly noted for its distinguished mathematicians and scientists. One of them was Euclid, whose book on geometry is still used in many schools today; it is easily the world's oldest school textbook. Another named Eratosthenes worked out the size of the earth by the use of geometry, and arrived remarkably close to the correct answer. The same man made an accurate map of the world as it was then known. As you will see, this map not only marks Britain, but shows it as being roughly the correct size and shape.

Then there were the great astronomers, Aristarchus and, later, Ptolemy. Aristarchus maintained that the earth revolved round the sun. But Ptolemy, like Aristotle before him, thought that the earth was the centre of the universe, and that the sun and all the stars revolved around us. Throughout the Middle Ages men blindly accepted what Ptolemy had said; but in the sixteenth century, it was proved that Aristarchus was right after all. (See *A History of Britain*, vol. 2, page 149.)

Another famous scientist was Hero, the inventor of the first steam turbine; and Archimedes, who discovered the lever and the law of Specific Gravity, visited Alexandria too. Here was a late but splendid flowering of classical science. In fact, not until modern times was this 'great blaze of knowledge and discovery' to be equalled anywhere in the world.

Perhaps, after all, as much good as evil came out of Alexander's thirteen terrible years of bloodshed and conquest. Certainly, the Macedonians differed from most of the earlier empire-builders in one important respect: they carried a higher, and not a lower, standard of civilization with them.

The rise of Rome

Alexander's conquests had spread Greek civilization into the heart of the east. Meanwhile, in Europe, another military power was rising which was destined to carry the same ideas as far to the west: this was the power of Rome.

We first hear of Rome as a small trading city about half-way up the 'leg' of Italy, on its western side. The people of this tiny state were Indo-Europeans who spoke the Latin language. Originally they had been governed by kings. But about 500 B.C. the monarch was expelled, and Rome became an oligarchy. This meant that she was ruled by her nobles, who debated and kept control of affairs through a council known as the Senate.

In Greece oligarchy was followed by democracy, or the rule of the citizens. At Rome the ordinary citizens struggled hard for political influence and eventually won the right to hold their own popular Assembly, as well as other important privileges. But the Senate of nobles and wealthy citizens kept the real power in their own hands. So Rome never became a true democracy in the Greek sense.

During the 6th century B.C., Rome was a little state, surrounded by other states of equal importance. But gradually, under the rule of the Senate, she began to extend her government over the neighbouring peoples. By the time of Alexander the Great, she had conquered the whole of central Italy and made herself the strongest power in the western Mediterranean – or, at least, the strongest but one.

Rome's rival was Carthage, on the coast of north Africa. This Phoenician city had grown extremely rich and powerful on the profits of her overseas trade. Moreover, like the Romans themselves, the Carthaginians were ambitious. They had already built up an empire which included Sicily, Corsica, Sardinia, and southern Spain. There was not enough room for two such powers – or so each of them thought. It became a question of Rome, or Carthage.

To settle this issue, the rivals fought each other for over a hundred years, in a series of wars known as the Punic Wars: one of the longest and bitterest struggles of all history. Several times it seemed that the Romans would be defeated, particularly when the Carthaginian general Hannibal surprised them in the rear, by taking a train of elephants through Spain and France, and over the Alps. But nothing could overcome the steadfast determination and resolute will of the Romans. In the end, they were victorious, and Carthage was burnt to the ground (146 B.C.).

One of Hannibal's elephants as shown on an Italian vase of the 3rd century B.C.

160

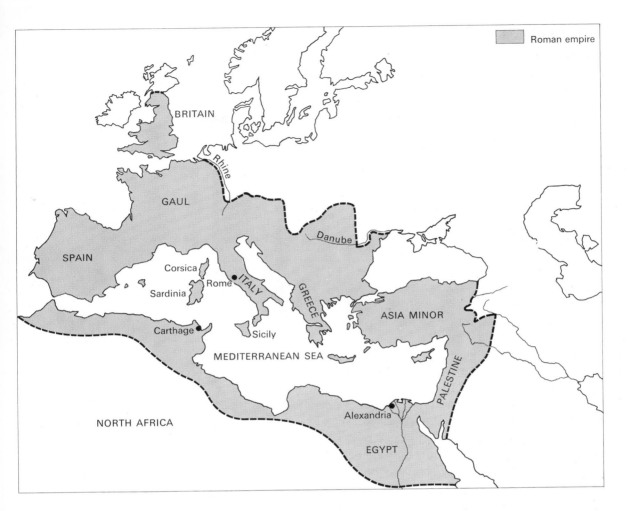

The Roman empire at its largest extent in the 2nd century A.D. This map does not name the Roman provinces but merely shows the countries included in the empire.

After this, it was not long before Rome had gained control of most of the lands round the Mediterranean, including north Africa, Egypt, Gaul, Spain, Palestine, Asia Minor, and Greece.

Unfortunately, Rome was no longer mistress of herself. When the fighting was over and the new provinces won, the Senate and people quickly found that they were unable to control the soldiers who had won them. From about 100 B.C. to 50 B.C., first one general and then another marched on the capital and made a great massacre of any who dared oppose him. The sword Rome had forged was pointed at her own heart. Unrest and civil war reigned everywhere.

History proves that there is only one answer to a desperate situation of this kind. The fighting and bloodshed can only be stopped when one person is strong enough to take complete power

The *testudo* (tortoise), a formation in which Roman soldiers held their shields over their heads, sometimes to charge, sometimes to protect mining or ramming operations.

Julius Caesar. What kind of man does he seem to be from this contemporary, or near contemporary, portrait? Does the face show, for instance, intelligence, cunning, ambition or determination?

into his own hands – and keep it. He does not allow the citizens to have any say in matters of government.

Julius Caesar was the first to seize power in this way. He was a ruthless and ambitious man, but one of the ablest soldiers and politicians there has ever been. To begin with, he built up his strength and reputation by conquering Gaul (or France). Then, in 49 B.C. at the head of his legions, Caesar marched on Rome. Within a short time he had won control over the Senate and had himself made dictator, or sole ruler, for life.

In a last desperate effort to save the old Roman 'freedom', a group of conspirators stabbed Caesar to death (44 B.C.). But this deed could not prevent the inevitable from happening. Its only result was a further thirteen years of fighting among the rival generals. When this was over, the victorious general stood in the same position which Caesar had held before: one man was again in complete control. This new ruler was Julius Caesar's nephew, Octavian, who, in 27 B.C. received the title of Augustus, and became in effect the first Roman emperor.

Augustus made a pretence of governing in partnership with the Senate, but in fact from this time onwards the citizens of Rome ceased to have any say in matters of government; all real power passed into the hands of the emperors, who – like Alexander earlier – demanded that subject peoples should worship them as gods. Nothing could be further removed from the ideas of democracy. Citizens did not even have the chance to choose the supreme ruler. When one emperor died or – as more often happened – was stabbed or poisoned, the strongest man usually seized control, just as Caesar had done. Sometimes several people claimed the imperial purple at the same time, which led to a further bout of civil war. Many of the later emperors were not Roman by blood; they were Spaniards, Africans, Arabs – their only right to the throne was the might of the legions supporting them.

What the Romans achieved

This does not sound the sort of empire which would last 500 years; which would bring long periods of peace and prosperity, like the golden age of the Antonine emperors; which would make men of many different countries and races proud to call themselves Roman citizens. Yet the Roman empire did all these things. It is difficult to understand why. Perhaps the main reason is that the Romans, despite their limitations, had an unrivalled gift for just and wise government.

From the start, Augustus Caesar organized the empire on sound lines. Like the Persian empire, it was divided into areas called provinces, each ruled by its own governor who was appointed by the emperor himself. A governor had many lesser officials to help in the efficient running of his territory, like present-day civil servants. He also had a permanent garrison of troops, so that he could protect the province, and maintain peace and order.

The people of each province had to pay taxes to Rome, abide by Roman Law and obey the commands of the governor. Latin

Augustus Caesar. Compare this and the portrait of Julius Caesar with the more formal, stylized portraits of the early civilizations (chapters 3–6). The Roman period saw the perfection of realistic lifelike portraiture, but most of the sculptors were either Greek or of Greek training.

Paying taxes to Rome in Augusta Treverorum (modern Trèves, in France). The peasants (in local dress) had to pay in kind as well as in cash.

was the official language. Everywhere, the governor ensured that the natives built towns and cities on the Roman pattern, with a market-place, a town hall, public baths, schools, shops, temples and Roman-type houses. Thus the natives were gradually civilized and encouraged to live in the Roman style. In modern times, Britain spread the western 'way of life' in a similar manner throughout the countries of her empire.

But the Romans did not only 'Romanize'. Part of their secret was to show respect for the peoples they had conquered. As in Alexander's empire, each district and city was allowed to elect its own local officials, and carry on its own local government. Naturally, the natives were forbidden to do anything which went against the wishes of Rome; but as far as possible, they were trusted by the governor, and left to themselves.

Another way in which the Romans showed respect for the conquered peoples was by gradually extending the rights of Roman

Above: a Roman meal. Two slaves in the wine cellar fill goblets and then serve the couple seated at the table on which stands a plate of fish. The woman has a fruit-basket on her lap. Women usually sat at table; men reclined.

A butcher's shop. The butcher is preparing chops. Note the various other types of meat for sale. Can you identify some of them? Note also the scales (*right*), and the seated customer (*left*). How different is the Roman butcher's chopper from the ones in use today?

Above: a draper's shop. Two customers of rank sit with their personal slaves on either side of them, while shop assistants hold up a large piece of cloth.

A cutler's shop, with sickles and several sorts of knives. The two main types of male clothing can be seen. The customer *(left)* wears a toga, the distinctive dress of Roman citizens. The cutler *(right)* is in a short-sleeved tunic.

citizenship to them; until in A.D. 212 all free men throughout the empire were admitted to full citizenship.

It is true that Roman citizenship amounted to very little, when compared to the privileges which the Greeks had enjoyed, or even those we have as citizens of a modern democracy. As already pointed out, the Roman citizen could have no say whatever in the government of the empire.

Nevertheless, citizenship did carry important advantages. It ensured that a person was paid proper respect as a free individual. No one could ill-treat or bully a Roman citizen with impunity, for the citizen could claim the full protection of the Roman Law and the Roman state. That is why, when St Paul was being harshly or unjustly treated on his missionary journeys, he only had to mention the fact that he was a citizen of Rome, and the attitude of the local magistrates immediately changed. There were things you could not say or do to a Roman citizen.

In the past, the empires of the east had consisted of the governing race on the one hand, and on the other, subject peoples who had few rights, and little or no protection against ill-treatment. But Rome had the very different idea of taking conquered peoples into full partnership. In this way, she bound all the members of

A chariot race. The driver has just come to the turning point marked by the three pyramidal columns. Going round this at speed required great skill and, when several chariots were bunched together, could be highly dangerous. The charioteer has the reins wrapped round his body; he carried a knife with which to cut them if the chariot overturned.

Roman relief showing a fight in the arena between gladiators and wild beasts. In the box on the left are spectators, while the rack in the middle holds seven eggs, one of which was removed after each event. Scenes like this were staged every day in the Colosseum for the Roman people.

Coin showing the Roman Colosseum.

her empire together, and made them loyal to herself. Undoubtedly, this was one of the main reasons the empire lasted as long as it did.

Rome did much for the provinces she ruled. With her strong armies and efficient civil servants, she brought them peace, security and order. By minting large quantities of coinage, and linking one part of the empire to another, she greatly encouraged trade. Above all, to many countries which had known nothing of the kind before, Rome brought the rich heritage of the ancient civilizations. As we shall see in the next chapter, one such country was Britain.

It is not easy to be fond of the Romans of the empire period. On the whole, they were far less civilized than the Greeks, being savage and brutal at heart. Consider, for instance, what they did with the Greek theatre. They turned it into an amphitheatre. Plays were never very popular at Rome, so they staged gladiatorial contests, baited wild animals, threw slaves and Christians to the lions.

Many educated Romans had higher standards than this and did their best to preserve and popularize classical Greek culture. The poet Horace told his friends to 'read the Greek masterpieces, thumb them day and night'. The architect, Vitruvius, studied Greek temples, leaving a careful record of many that have since perished. Roman sculptors made accurate and loving copies of famous Greek statues, but for which fact some works would have been totally lost to us. Myron's *Discus Thrower*, illustrated on page 139 is a Roman copy, the original having disappeared. The same applies to the portraits of Pericles and Socrates on pages 134 and 145.

The Romans produced great writers of their own: poets like Virgil, Horace and Ovid; historians like Livy and Tacitus; orators like Cicero. The writings of such men are still widely read today and serve as an enduring monument to all that was best in the Roman character.

Nevertheless, the Romans lacked the brilliant imagination and the creative power of the Greeks. No Latin poet quite compares with Homer; no Latin philosopher influenced the future like Socrates. The Romans made hardly any important scientific discoveries, for they were without the eager curiosity of men like Anaxagoras and Aristotle. In matters of the mind and spirit, they could never equal the Greeks.

Yet the Romans had a genius of their own. Their genius was for practical things. The Greeks thought; the Romans did.

They were great law-makers. Early peoples had regarded the law as something which came from above. Hammurabi's Pillar (page 96) shows him receiving authority from the Babylonian Sun-god, while the Bible tells how Jehovah gave the Ten Commandments to Moses on Mount Sinai. Laws which come from above tend to be regarded as unalterable, which is indeed what the Jews felt about their laws. But the Romans thought that laws ought to be changed as society changes, and that, instead of accepting an unalterable code from some higher power, men themselves ought always to be striving to improve their laws and make them more just. For over a thousand years Roman lawyers were striving to do this. And so fine was Roman Law by the time they had finished that it continued to be used throughout most of Europe for a further thousand years. Even today in many countries the study of Roman Law remains an essential part of every lawyer's training.

Architecture interested the Romans because it was practical; they developed the classical style by adding to it the vault, the semicircular arch and the dome. They built in brick, as well as stone, and also mastered the art of using concrete. The domed roof of the Pantheon at Rome is 140 feet across and is a single

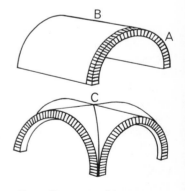

Above: Roman architecture. The semicircular arch (A), when extended over a distance, produced the semicircular vault (B). The Romans also devised a clever way of managing the intersection, when they wished two semicircular vaults to cross each other (C). These architectural features were used during the early Middle Ages.

The Roman Colosseum today, where gladiator fights were held (see page 163). Built in A.D. 80, it could accommodate nearly 50,000 people.

Below: aqueduct at Segovia in Spain. This crosses a valley in the middle of the city. The watercourse is at the top and brings water from springs ten miles away.

piece of concrete. After 1,800 years this dome is as safe as on the day it was built.

The ability of the Romans as engineers was no less remarkable. They gave the empire a superb network of broad, straight roads, with hard permanent surfaces. They built amazing bridges and aqueducts; many of them stand today; a few are still in use.

On a smaller scale, we cannot help but admire the Romans for their lettering, the influence of which is still very much with us.

Roman transport.
Above: Roman coach, drawn by a pair of horses. What other types of land transport did the Romans have?
Below: Roman merchant ship, similar to the type used by the Phoenicians (see page 105) except that it appears to have been only a sailing vessel, since, apart from the steering oar, no others are shown. The sail is called a lateen sail and is still used in the Mediterranean today.

Classic Roman lettering was designed to be inscribed on stone slabs, which were often set high over a doorway or on a triumphal arch. Fancy ornamentation was avoided, for this would have made the inscriptions difficult to read at a distance. Instead the Romans kept their letters as plain as possible, producing forms that were bold, clear and dignified. As you will see from the illustration on page 185, the classic Roman letters provide the basis of our own 'printed' capitals.

The practical flair of the Romans showed itself in everything they touched. So did their sound judgement, their common sense, and their thoroughness. It was these qualities that built and maintained the Roman empire. Virgil, perhaps the greatest of the Roman poets, shows himself to be fully aware both of the limitations and the unique gifts of his people in the following passage:

A coin design devised by the Greeks (top), copied by the Romans (centre), and eventually introduced on to English coins by Charles II (bottom).

Others, no doubt, will better mould the bronze
To the semblance of soft breathing, draw from marble
The living countenance; and others plead
With greater eloquence, or learn to measure,
Better than we, the pathways of the heaven,
The risings of the stars; remember, Roman,
To rule the people under law, to establish
The way of peace, to battle down the haughty,
To spare the meek. Our fine arts, these, forever.

From the Greeks modern Western civilization has inherited its love of learning and beauty and political freedom; from the Hebrews we have inherited our conscience and our religion; from Rome we have inherited our love of justice and order, and our ability – whatever the difficulties – to get things done.

Dates to remember

323 B.C.   Death of Alexander the Great
146 B.C.   The burning of Carthage
 44 B.C.   Julius Caesar assassinated
 27 B.C.   Augustus Caesar becomes the first Roman emperor

Things to do

1   Read some of the legendary stories associated with Alexander the Great. What sort of picture do they give of him? What has to be remembered on the other side?
2   Collect together all the information you can about Archimedes.
3   Look up the name Hannibal in encyclopedias and reference books. Make a summary of what you discover about him.
4   Find out what you can about the ancient city of Rome, with particular reference to its architecture. Make drawings of some of its famous buildings.

Books to read

Naomi Mitchison, *Alexander the Great*, Longmans
N. Sherwin-White, *Ancient Rome*, Longmans
H. A. Treble and K. M. King, *Everyday Life in Rome*, Oxford University Press
F. R. Cowell, *Everyday Life in Ancient Rome*, Batsford

Chapter 10
Civilization reaches Britain

In this chapter we shall see how the Romans brought civilization to our own country. But first something must be said about the course of events in earlier times. From the days of the Roman empire, we must go back several thousand years.

The New Stone Age

The New Stone Age, which began in the Near East about 8000 B.C., did not reach Britain until after 3500 B.C. By that time Sumer and Egypt had become highly civilized lands, yet the inhabitants of Britain remained primitive hunters, depending for their livelihood on the killing of wild animals, fishing, and the gathering of wild fruits.

A people enter the New Stone Age when they begin to practise farming. How was this advance made in Britain?

It was not made by the native hunters, but by settlers from overseas. They came between 3500 B.C. and 3000 B.C. from the mainland of Europe. When they crossed the Channel in their small boats, they carried cargoes of cattle, sheep and seed-corn with them.

The Britain they found was very different from the one we know today. At this time, and for long afterwards, much of the island was covered by thick forest. However, some parts of it were easier to clear than others.

In particular there were the chalk and limestone hills, where the land was well drained and there were comparatively few trees. Such uplands lie like a great hand over southern England. The palm of the hand is Salisbury Plain; its fingers are the Cotswolds, the Chiltern Hills, the North and the South Downs. Other suitable hills were in Wales and northern England.

In such areas Britain's earliest farmers seem to have lived in rectangular huts made of wood. Round their settlements they cleared small plots of land, and sowed wheat and barley on Britain's first cornfields. But more important than their crops were the large herds of cattle on which their prosperity depended, together with pigs, goats and sheep. These were Britain's earliest farm animals.

The Chiltern Hills are of chalk and extend through East Anglia to Norfolk, whilst the limestone ridge of the Cotswolds continues in the Northampton Uplands, the Lincoln Edge and the Yorkshire Wolds. Away from the chalk and limestone most of prehistoric south-eastern England was either marsh or heavy oak forest, and therefore unfavourable for settlement. There were fewer trees in the north-west but it was colder and damper with less fertile soil.

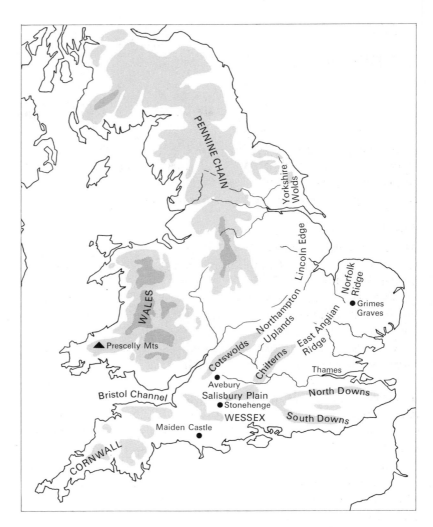

A bowl and a spoon made by Britain's first farmers. The bag-like shape of these early pots suggests that they may have been copies in clay of leather containers.

In Britain, as in the Near East, the New Stone Age meant not only the introduction of farming but also of several new crafts. The first farmers were the earliest inhabitants of this country to make pottery (see illustration left). They may also have been weavers, though this has not been proved.

Certainly, like other New Stone Age peoples, they were highly skilled at making flint and stone implements. Their axes were quite different from those of earlier times. After the axe-head had been chipped into shape, its surface was rubbed on a wetted stone slab until it had a polished appearance (see page 171).

These polished axe-heads, which were fitted into handles, were extremely important to the New Stone Age peoples, because they needed them for land clearance. Great trouble was taken to obtain

173

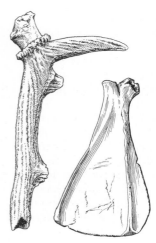

Above left: deer antler used as a pick in flint mining at Grime's Graves. *Right:* shoulder blade of an ox used as a shovel.

Left: a flint pit at Grime's Graves, Norfolk.

the best materials. At places like Grime's Graves in Norfolk top quality flints were dug out from underground mines, using deer antlers as picks and the shoulder-blades of cattle as shovels.

But various types of volcanic stone found in the west of Britain made even better axe-heads. Today when one of these axe-heads is excavated a thin section is cut from it. By examining this under a microscope, geologists can tell where the stone originally came from. As a result we now know that there were a number of 'axe-factories' from which axe-heads were sent all over the country (see map opposite). The flint and stone axe industries of the New Stone Age were an early British trade.

Generally the early farmers buried their dead in long barrows. These were great mounds of earth, anything from 30 to over 100 yards in length, with one end higher and wider than the other. Inside many long barrows there are burial chambers constructed of large blocks of stone, with a passage giving access from outside. Such tombs were re-opened as occasion required and burials were placed in them over many centuries. Probably they were the family vaults of chieftains and other influential people.

Long barrows can be seen in Ireland, in many parts of Scotland and Wales, and on the chalk and limestone hills of England.

'Goddess' figure of the New Stone Age, carved out of a lump of chalk and found at Grime's Graves. Compare with illustration on page 31.

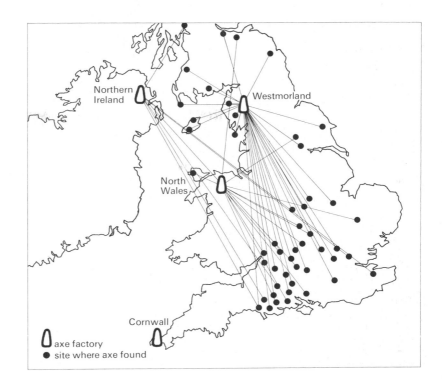

Above: polished axe head found in Lincolnshire but probably made at an axe factory in Westmorland.
Right: the main axe factories in New Stone Age Britain with lines radiating to places where axes from them have been discovered. The distribution of Cornish axes is not shown, since they have been found throughout the country.

Northern Ireland

Westmorland

North Wales

Cornwall

⊓ axe factory
● site where axe found

West Kennet Long Barrow, Wiltshire. This view, taken from just inside the entrance of the tomb, shows the long passageway, built of huge stone blocks. Burial chambers can be seen opening off from right and left, with a final chamber at the far end.

The Bronze Age

In about 1850 B.C. bands of settlers began arriving from the Continent who had a knowledge of metals. Archaeologists call them the Beaker folk because of the beaker-shaped pots which are frequently excavated among their remains. In graves of the Beaker folk various metal objects have been found, such as copper axe-heads, knives and daggers, and small discs and ear-rings of gold. These are Britain's oldest metal articles.

Most likely it was the Beaker folk who began mining the copper and gold ores of Wales and Ireland. Before long, too, metal-smiths somehow discovered that, by adding a little tin to the copper, they could produce a tougher metal, bronze.

The making of bronze had begun in the Near East about 3500 B.C. By about 1700 B.C. bronze tools and weapons were sufficiently common for us to speak of Britain as entering the Bronze Age.

During our early Bronze Age southern Britain was dominated by the wealthy and powerful chieftains of Wessex. Ireland, Wales and Cornwall were now important centres of the metal industry, and the Wessex chieftains gained control of this trade, exporting much British metal-work to the mainland of Europe. Out of the profits they were able to bring back many rare and costly things: amber from the Baltic, gold objects which could have come from Mycenaean Greece, and small blue beads which must have come from Egypt.

In contrast to the New Stone Age peoples, men of the Bronze Age generally buried their dead in round barrows; and it is in such graves that archaeologists discover the precious possessions of the Wessex chieftains.

It was during the late New Stone Age and the early Bronze Age that the world-famous prehistoric temples of Avebury and Stonehenge were built. The open air temple at Avebury is so vast that a village now stands in the middle of it.

It consisted of a Great Circle of about a hundred upright stones, some of them weighing 40 tons. Inside this were two smaller circles, while outside it, surrounding the whole temple, was a circular ditch and outer bank, 1,400 feet in diameter. From the main entrance, an avenue of large stones ran for over a mile southwards, to a much smaller sanctuary on a neighbouring hill.

How the huge stones were transported and raised into position no one knows. The Avebury stones had only to be brought a few miles; but the bluestones used at Stonehenge, which weighed up to 4 tons each, were brought over 200 miles from the mountains of Pembrokeshire in Wales.

A beaker of the type associated with the Beaker folk, about 6 inches tall. The 'necked' shape was more difficult to make than the pot on page 169. New Stone Age pottery was undecorated, but Bronze Age beakers were usually 'engraved' with geometric designs.

A cluster of round barrows at Lambourne in Berkshire, seen from the air.

176

Avebury. The houses in the
aerial photograph give some
idea of the scale, while the
reconstruction below suggests
how it looked in prehistoric
times. Many of the stones
have now disappeared, but a
good number belonging to the
Great Circle can be seen on
the right of the photograph.

There can be little doubt that the people who built these places of worship, and smaller ones like them in other parts of Britain, were deeply religious; but, again, nobody knows what their religion was.

Stonehenge is much smaller than Avebury, and in some ways less impressive. On the other hand, it is justly renowned as being the first major work of architecture in this country. At Avebury the rocks were left in their natural form; but at Stonehenge they were painstakingly shaped into regular blocks of uniform size. Moreover, as you will see from the illustration below, the outer ring of thirty uprights was originally capped by a continuous circle of lintel stones, each curved and angled so that it would fit perfectly. Nor did the lintels merely rest on top of the

Stonehenge. On the right is the outer circle of uprights, with their curved lintel stones, some of which have now fallen. On the left is one of the five trilithons. Between the outer ring and the trilithon, a smaller upright can be seen. This is one of at least 60 bluestones from Pembrokeshire which formed a second circle.

Mortice and tenon joints at Stonehenge. A tenon can be seen on the top of the upright, and a mortice hole on the fallen stone in the bottom right-hand corner. (See also the caption on page 114.)

Progress in metal-working. *Left:* an early open axe-mould, suitable for casting copper. *Centre and right:* a two-piece mould of the sort used later for casting bronze axe-heads. *Centre:* the inside of one half of the mould; *right:* the outside, when the two pieces were bound together, before pouring in molten metal through the funnel at the top.

uprights; they were keyed into them by accurately made mortice and tenon joints (see illustration left). Inside this continuous circle, the horse-shoe of five trilithons was constructed in a similar way: each trilithon consisting of two upright stones, with a third placed across the top. Stonehenge was not a primitive stone circle, but a true building.

The Iron Age

Soon after 500 B.C. the use of iron began in this country – 700 years after the Near East had entered its Iron Age.

During this period an Indo-European people called the Celts invaded Britain. They came from Gaul (now Belgium and France), and took possession of the warmer and more fertile south-east, pushing the natives to the west and north.

For information about the inhabitants of Britain so far, we have had to depend entirely on the discoveries of archaeologists, since no written record exists to tell us what they were like. Now, however, there at last begin for our own island those writings that turn prehistory into history (see page 8). Julius Caesar, who twice invaded Britain (in 55 and 54 B.C.), left a description of the Celts in his book, *The Conquest of Gaul*. He tells us that:

Most of the tribes of the interior do not grow corn but live on milk and meat, and wear skins. All the Britons dye their bodies with woad, which produces a blue colour, and this gives them a more terrifying appearance in battle. They wear their hair long, and shave the whole of their bodies except the head and the upper lip.

The Celts were a warlike people and greatly impressed Caesar with their skilful use of the chariot:

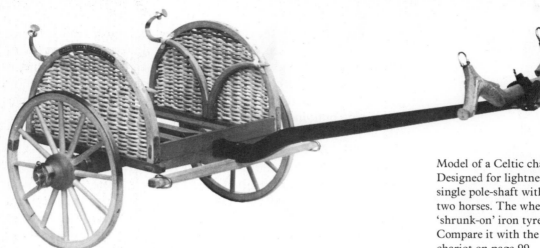

Model of a Celtic chariot. Designed for lightness, it had a single pole-shaft with yokes for two horses. The wheels had 'shrunk-on' iron tyres. Compare it with the Hittite chariot on page 99.

Right: hill fort at Maiden Castle, Dorset, seen from the air. This was probably the capital of a local Celtic tribe. Its defences enclose an area of 45 acres. (The white lines inside the fort mark the excavations of archaeologists.)

In chariot fighting the Britons begin by driving all over the field hurling javelins, and generally the terror inspired by the horses and the noise of the wheels are sufficient to throw their opponents' ranks into disorder. Then . . . they jump down from the chariots and engage on foot. In the meantime their charioteers retire a short distance from the battle and place the chariots in such a position that their masters, if hard pressed by numbers, have an easy means of retreat to their own lines . . . by daily training and practice they attain such proficiency that even on a steep incline they are able to control the horses at full gallop, and to check and turn them in a moment. They can run along the chariot pole, stand on the yoke, and get back into the chariot as quick as lightning.

Some Iron Age Britons lived in isolated farmsteads (see opposite), but others in hill-top villages which, in times of war, served as forts. They can be seen crowning many hills today, and are well worth exploring. The early ones have a single bank and ditch, but during the 1st century, forts were often given multiple ramparts, like the famous one at Maiden Castle, Dorset, which is protected by a series of four banks and ditches, with maze-like entrances at the east and west ends.

Excavations suggest that in the middle of a typical hill-village, there would be a timber enclosure where sheep and cattle were penned for the night. The houses of the inhabitants were circular, with conical roofs made of turf or thatch. Each contained a single room which had an open hearth at its centre. For furniture there might be one or two rough-hewn stools, a simple table, and a bed covered with hides. For cooking there were pots and pans, and perhaps a bronze cauldron; while each family possessed a few iron tools and weapons.

Right: reconstruction of an Iron Age farmstead at Little Woodbury, near Salisbury. The circular farmhouse was unusually large, about 50 feet in diameter. In the stockaded farmyard can be seen corn-drying racks, hay-poles and (extreme right) granaries for the storing of seed corn. Bread corn was kept in the farm silos, or grain storage pits.

Every village had its own headman, who lived in a larger house than the rest, was better dressed, and wore richer ornaments. He might have a ceremonial bronze helmet and shield, or even a gold torc to wear round his neck.

The metal-smiths of Celtic Britain made objects of bronze and gold that are true works of art, so that things like the Battersea Shield and the Desborough Mirror are among our most treasured national possessions. These you could see in the British Museum.

As well as being farmers, the Britons did a great deal of trading, both between themselves, and with the peoples of Europe. Among British exports were corn, cattle, iron, hides and slaves. The Celtic tribes of southern Britain minted their own coins, while others used bars of iron for money.

Celtic metal-work. *Top left:* engraved back of a bronze mirror found at Desborough, Northants. The front is of polished bronze. *Below left:* torc, or necklace made of electrum, an alloy of silver and gold, found at Snettisham, Norfolk. *Below:* part of a shield found in the Thames at Battersea. This was made for ceremonial purposes—not to fight with but to impress.

Two coins showing a horse.
Top: Celtic. Bottom: Roman.

From the continent the Celts were already bringing back Roman wine, Roman pottery and Roman metal-work. But they were soon to have more things Roman than they bargained for.

The Roman conquest of Britain

Once Gaul had been added to the Roman empire the addition of Britain was more or less inevitable. Close ties existed between the Celtic tribes of the two countries, and whenever the Gauls wished to make trouble for the Romans they could be sure of help from their friends across the Channel. Caesar himself gave as his main reason for invading this country the fact that 'in almost all the Gallic campaigns the Gauls received reinforcements from the Britons'.

But the Romans hoped that the conquest would prove worthwhile from other points of view. The south-east was prosperous and should be able to pay high taxes into the Imperial treasury, while Britain was known to be rich in tin, iron-ore, and other valuable minerals.

Caesar's invasions of 55 and 54 B.C. are fully described in *The Conquest of Gaul*. On the first occasion he tried to land his army of about 10,000 men near Deal in Kent. But the Romans were met by a large force of natives and, due to the gradual slope of the beach, could not get their ships close in shore. For a moment the legionaries seemed daunted by the prospect of having to wade through deep water and at the same time fight against the determined Britons. But then, Caesar tells us:

the man who carried the eagle of the 10th legion, after praying to the gods that his action might bring good luck to the legions, cried in a loud voice: 'Jump down, comrades, unless you want to surrender to the enemy; I, at any rate, mean to do my duty to my country and my general.' With these words he leapt out of the ship and advanced towards the enemy with the eagle in his hands. At this the soldiers, exhorting each other not to submit to such disgrace, jumped with one accord from the ship, and the men from the next ships, when they saw them, followed them and advanced against the enemy.

But, despite such acts of heroism, Caesar's expeditions did not lead to the takeover of Britain; it was not until A.D. 43, during the reign of the Emperor Claudius, that the real conquest began.

Again the Britons put up a fight. A Roman army of over 40,000 had captured the south-east lowlands by A.D. 47, building the 170 mile road, called the Fosse Way, from Lincoln to Exeter, as a temporary frontier. But the tribes of the north and west resisted fiercely, so that it took the Romans another forty years to

Barbarian with a shield. This little statuette comes from Roman London.

bring Wales and northern England under full military control. The Picts – the people who then inhabited Scotland – were never conquered. Instead, about A.D. 120, the Emperor Hadrian had to order the building of Hadrian's Wall, to prevent them from raiding across the imperial frontier. This ran for seventy-three miles, from the Tyne estuary to the Solway Firth (see map on page 191). Much of it still stands today.

Britain under the Romans

As a province of the empire, Britain was ruled by a Roman governor, who was both commander-in-chief of the army and head of the civil government.

In the north-west highlands which had proved so difficult to conquer, there was little fertile land, and insufficient wealth for the building of cities. The Romans studded the countryside with permanent military forts, leaving three legions – based on Caerleon, Chester and York – to police the area, and see that the barbarian tribes caused as little trouble as possible. Otherwise the natives were left to carry on the same way of life as before.

In the lowlands the situation was different. Here there was plenty of good farming land. Here also, after the defeat of Boudicca's revolt in A.D. 61, the Celts soon showed themselves willing to accept imperial rule. Thus, having conquered the southerners, the Romans were able to set about civilizing them.

This they did with their usual good judgement and common sense. The Britons, before their defeat, had lived in independent tribes, each ruling itself from its own capital. Afterwards they were allowed to go on managing local affairs in the same groups.

However, they had to pay Roman taxes, and obey the orders of the Roman governor. Then, too, they were compelled to leave their old tribal capitals. Usually these had been heavily fortified strongholds, on some remote and formidable hilltop. But now each tribe had to build a new capital on lower ground, where they would find it less easy to stage a revolt.

Moreover, because the Romans wished to civilize the Britons, they encouraged them to build these new centres, not as clusters of primitive huts, but as true Roman cities. The map opposite shows the tribal districts into which Roman Britain was divided, and also marks the city that served each as its capital.

Let us look at one of these cities in the 2nd century A.D., when the prosperity of Roman Britain was at its height.

In Shropshire, five miles south-east of Shrewsbury, there is a quiet little village called Wroxeter. Today, it is just a church

A man and child wearing the Roman toga. Compare with illustrations on pages 160 and 161. This relief is on a tombstone, probably from London.

Roman Britain, showing
the tribal areas (and their
approximate boundaries),
and the main towns.

Key

1 Damnonii
2 Votadini
3 Selgovae
4 Novantae
5 Brigantes
6 Parisi
7 Ordovices
8 Cornovii
9 Coritani
10 Iceni
11 Demetae
12 Dobunni
13 Catuvellauni
14 Trinovantes
15 Silures
16 Atrebates
17 Belgae
18 Cantiaci
19 Regnenses
20 Durotriges
21 Dumnonii

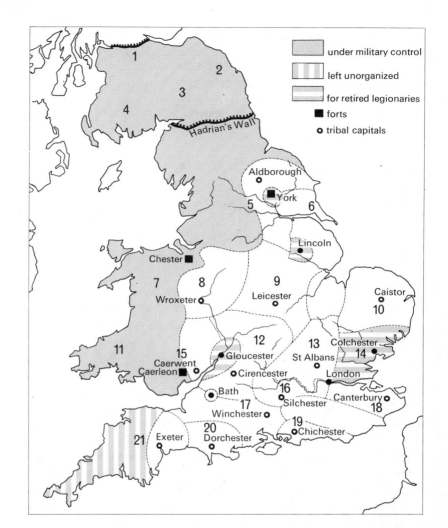

and a few houses. Yet, at this place, there stood once the proud
Viroconium, fourth largest city in Roman Britain.

Viroconium was the capital of the Cornovii tribe. In Celtic
times, their old headquarters had been on the top of the Wrekin,
a great whale-backed hill close by. But now the new capital stood
on the banks of the River Severn, where this is crossed by
the main Roman road to central Wales.

Viroconium, which had a population of about 6,000, was
roughly oval in shape, and occupied an area of 180 acres. Much
of the city had been town-planned from the beginning. It was
laid out in large rectangular building blocks with straight roads
and crossroads generally at right-angles. Surrounding it was a
stone wall, 20 feet high, and a ditch 60 feet wide.

Above: reconstruction of the Roman south-east gate at St Albans. It was built of stone, but, as is usual with Roman masonry, had 'binding courses' of red tiles every few feet.

Left: sketch-plan of Viroconium as it has so far been revealed by excavation and aerial photography. You can guess the likely position of the gates by the gaps in the defences.

The gateways at Wroxeter have not yet been excavated; but Roman cities generally had between four and six. The illustration above shows what a typical gateway looked like.

Entering Viroconium from the south, we would find that the main street ran in a straight line towards the centre of the city. On either side was an interesting variety of buildings.

The town houses of the wealthy tribal nobles would certainly catch the eye. They were large, stone-fronted mansions, standing some way back from the road in their own grounds. Inside, they had plastered walls, with brightly coloured patterns on them; while perhaps, decorating the floors of the main rooms, there would be fine mosaic pavements. Some of the floors had heating chambers called hypocausts beneath them for warming the rooms by the Roman system of central heating.

Apart from these particularly imposing houses, there were many smaller ones, the property of the town's merchants and office workers.

We would also pass a fair number of shops, which were long, narrow buildings, with one of the narrow ends set on to the street. Roman shops had no shop window; only a large open counter, such as you might see in a modern greengrocer's or

Opposite page

Above: eastern colonnade of the forum at Wroxeter as it is today, with the entrance marked by an arrow. *Below:* reconstruction of the forum in Roman times.

fishmonger's. They would be offering a wide variety of goods: pottery, whetstones, lamps and lamp oil, writing materials, jewellery, imported wines, as well as foodstuffs of various kinds.

Another building we would notice on our way to the city centre is the pagan temple. This had a courtyard in front, where several statues of gods and goddesses were probably set up. The temple itself was built in the classical style of architecture, which the Romans had learned from the Greeks, and were now teaching to the Britons.

By this time, we would be at the centre of the city which, in A.D. 200, must have been very impressive indeed. On our right would be the magnificent public bath building; while the long colonnaded front of the forum stretched away on the left.

Visitors to Wroxeter today can still see the bases of sixteen of the twenty-two pillars which formed the forum's colonnade. The twelfth and thirteenth columns are larger, and have a wider space between them than the others. This was the entrance, over which a splendid inscription dedicating the building to the Emperor Hadrian was erected (see opposite).

Had we passed through the entrance in Roman times, we would have found ourselves in a great open square which was the forum or market-place itself. Here all was noise and bustle. Here freemen and slaves came to do their shopping at the long lines of stalls set out in straight, parallel rows. They came not only from Viroconium, but from the farmsteads and villages round about, for as tribal capital, the town served a wide area. Nor was the forum only used for buying and selling. It was also the place where notices were displayed, where people met to gossip, where games and public meetings were held, and festivals celebrated. In fact, the heart of a Roman city was its forum.

At the far end of the market square we would see the basilica, or town hall. In layout, this building was similar to many of our churches. This is hardly surprising, since it was on the Roman basilica that the earliest Christian churches were later modelled. The basilica consisted of a nave and an east and west aisle. As in a church, between the nave and the aisles there was a colonnade of pillars, while the wall above was pierced by a line of windows known as the clerestory (or clear-story) which helped to light the nave. Both the column and the clerestory had been invented over 3,000 years before by the Egyptians (see page 68). Through the Romans, these and other civilized ideas had now reached Britain.

If the forum was the heart of Viroconium, the basilica was its head. The Cornovii tribe was governed by a tribal council.

Above: a roman leather sandal. Leather, unlike cloth, survives underground for a long time, so Roman shoes are frequently excavated.

Sketch plan of the forum and basilica at Wroxeter.

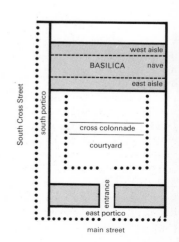

The forum inscription at Wroxeter. An abbreviated translation of the Latin reads: 'To the Emperor Caesar Trajanus Hadrianus Augustus ... Father of his Country, the Community of the Cornovii erected this building.'

This was made up of the most powerful and influential members of the tribe, and dealt with the day-to-day running of the town and surrounding countryside by the issuing of orders. In addition, local magistrates were chosen whose job it was to see that these orders were carried out and, where necessary, punish offenders. It was in the basilica that the tribal council met for its deliberations, and the magistrates held their law courts. Here also, civic receptions took place and important guests were entertained.

Across the road from the forum were the town baths, where a series of cold, warm and hot rooms with underfloor heating caused the bather to perspire freely. If you want to know what this way of bathing feels like and how effective it is, the best thing to do is to go to a Turkish bath (or talk to somebody who has been to one), for this is the Roman system. To the Roman, a visit to the public baths was more than a way of cleaning the body. It was one of his favourite means of relaxation: an opportunity to sunbathe, play games, or spend an hour or two with his friends.

A view of part of the baths at Wroxeter. The upstanding masonry on the left was the main entrance (though the square pillar is a modern reinforcement). The first room through the entrance was the *frigidarium* or cold room. Then came a series of rooms in which the temperature became hotter and hotter. The remains of the underlying heating chambers known as hypocausts are in the left foreground. (Compare page 187.)

In addition to the tribal capitals like Wroxeter, Roman Britain had other types of cities. Colchester, Lincoln, Gloucester and York were founded as places where retired legionaries could settle, and so enjoyed special privileges. Verulamium (St Albans) had similar rights, although it was a native town. Then there was London, which, with a population of 15,000 was the largest and most flourishing town of all.

Finally, there were many settlements that were classed as small towns. These had only a thousand or so inhabitants, and lacked the impressive buildings, and the vigorous social life, which were found in the more important centres.

Roman towns of every description were built on well chosen sites: at important river crossings, or other natural meeting points. For this reason, towns usually stand on the same sites today. A good number of our county towns – like Leicester, York, Gloucester and Lincoln – were founded as Roman cities.

You can often tell whether a modern town goes back to Roman times, just by looking at its name. The Latin word for a walled fort, the origin of many English towns, is 'castra'. Generally changed to 'chester', 'caster' or 'cester', this word still features in many English place-names.

The Roman theatre at Verulamium (St Albans). In essentials it was like ancient Greek theatres (see pages 140–41). The four mounds mark the position of wooden seats from which citizens of Verulamium, whether Roman officials or Britons, watched performances. Back-stage accommodation was provided by the long, narrow room behind the stage area.

Above: remains of a hypocaust and mosaic pavement at Bath.

Part of a Roman mosaic pavement from Horkstow, Lincolnshire, showing chariot racing.

Roman towns were linked together by an intricate network of major and minor roads. The most important were the three great roads radiating out from London. Running to York, and beyond this to Corbridge near Hadrian's Wall, was Ermine Street, now the Great North Road, or A1. Crossing England in a north-westerly direction, towards Chester, was the Watling Street, now the A5 The third road made for the south-west, through Silchester and Dorchester, to Exeter.

As everyone knows, Roman roads run as straight as a die for miles on end. They were built with masterly skill. The Romans understood exactly how to give them firm foundations by using different materials in a series of layers; they also provided good drainage. There are places – like Blackstone Edge in Lancashire – where you can still walk on a Roman road surface even today.

Roman roads had to be well constructed because they were much used. Troops moved along them; so, too, did the corn supplies for the northern garrisons. Officials used them to make sure that the land was properly governed. They were important to farmers, and to people engaged in industry and trade.

Along the main roads there were small settlements at regular intervals – usually about every fifteen miles. Here travellers could get a change of horses; and also refresh themselves, or have a night's lodging at an inn. Such settlements are called Posting Stations because, among other things, they served the Imperial Post, by means of which government instructions were sent all over the empire.

After the towns, the chief centres of civilized life were the villas. Most of these were farm-houses, surrounded by their own estates. About 600 villas have been discovered in the lowlands of England, and there were doubtless hundreds more. Some were quite small, but others contained thirty or forty rooms, complete with an elaborate system of central heating and all the luxuries which Roman architects could provide. Such places were the homes of wealthy country gentlemen who enjoyed a very high standard of living, and tried to do everything in the Roman style.

By A.D. 200, all over southern England, in the towns and the villas, there were large numbers of native people who were 'Romanized'. They spoke Latin (as well as Celtic), wore Roman clothes, worshipped Roman gods, kept Roman holidays and festivals, and enjoyed the rights of full Roman citizenship. Many probably felt that they were almost as Roman as the citizens of the Eternal City itself.

Ermine Way, north of Hungerford, Berkshire.

Main Roman roads in Britain.

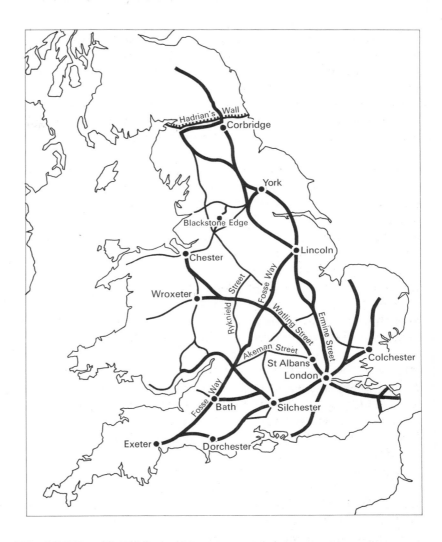

Roman road at Blackstone Edge, near Littleborough, Lancashire. This crossed the Pennines between Manchester and Ilkley. Paved with local stones, it is 16 feet wide. The sunken trough in the middle may have been turfed in Roman times to make the footing easier for horses hauling loads uphill.

Nevertheless, even in south-eastern England (not to mention Wales and the north) there were at least as many natives whose way of life had not become Roman. Away from the towns and the villas and the roads, were hundreds of British villages which had hardly changed at all since pre-Roman times. Here Roman things and Roman ways counted for very little. The people still spoke their own Celtic language, worshipped their own Celtic gods, and followed their own primitive customs.

So, although the Romans brought civilization to Britain, it cannot be said that they completely civilized it. Nor was the civilization they brought destined to last for ever.

Roman tableware from Wroxeter. *Above:* red-glazed pottery, made in imitation of bronze, and known as Samian ware. Such pottery, which was regarded as the 'best' tableware throughout the empire, was imported in bulk from the Continent. *Right:* locally made pottery: a flagon and a handled mug.

Dates to remember

3500–3000	B.C.	New Stone Age begins in Britain
about 1700	B.C.	Bronze Age begins
soon after 500	B.C.	Iron Age begins
A.D. 43		The Roman conquest begins

Things to do

1 Are there any prehistoric or Roman remains within thirty miles of your home? If so, make a map showing where they are (see caption to map opposite). Try to visit them.

2 Visit your local museum and see if it contains objects of pre-historic or Roman date. If so, make drawings and notes on some of the material.

3 Two Celtic leaders, Caractacus and Boudicca, are famous for their resistance to the Romans. From encyclopedias and other books, find out something about them.

4 Make a map of Britain and mark on all the towns which you know to be of Roman origin because of their names.

5 Decide which tribal area your home would have been in, had you lived in Roman times (see page 181). If you live in the south-east, find out all you can about your tribal capital (are there any excavated remains?). If you live in the north-west, find out about the nearest Roman town or fort.

6 Collect together as much information as possible on Roman roads and Roman methods of road-making.

7 From other books find out more either about Roman villas or Roman bath-houses. Make plans and drawings to show what the buildings were like; describe the system of heating which the Romans used.

8 One of the early governors of Roman Britain was a man called Agricola. In the passage below the Roman historian Tacitus describes how Agricola tried to civilize the natives.

To induce a people, hitherto scattered, uncivilized and therefore prone to fight, to grow pleasurably inured to peace and ease, Agricola gave private encouragement and official assistance to the building of temples, public squares and private mansions. . . . Furthermore, he trained the sons of the chiefs in the liberal arts. . . . The result was that in place of distaste for the Latin language came a passion to command it. In the same way, our national dress came into favour and the toga was everywhere to be seen.

(a) Find out the meaning of the following words: prone, inured, the liberal arts.
(b) What sort of buildings helped to civilize the Celtic Britons?
(c) Find out more about the toga, the national dress of the Romans.
(d) In modern times, what sort of buildings helped to civilize the natives of Nigeria and Ghana? What language did 'the sons of the chiefs' learn? Whose national dress did many of them adopt?

Ancient sites of prehistoric and Roman date are to be found throughout the country. If you want to know what can be seen in your area, the Ordnance Survey maps of Ancient Britain will tell you (England south of Scarborough and Wales are covered on the South Sheet). Below is part of the North Sheet showing Hadrian's Wall. The Ordnance Survey also publishes detailed maps of Britain in the Iron Age and Roman Britain.

Books to read

I. Doncaster, *Life in Prehistoric Times*, Longmans
R. R. Sellman, *Prehistoric Britain*, Methuen
I. Doncaster, *The Roman Occupation of Britain*, Longmans
R. R. Sellman, *Roman Britain*, Methuen
M. and C. H. B. Quennell, *Everyday Life in Prehistoric Times*, Batsford
M. and C. H. B. Quennell, *Everyday Life in Roman Britain*, Batsford

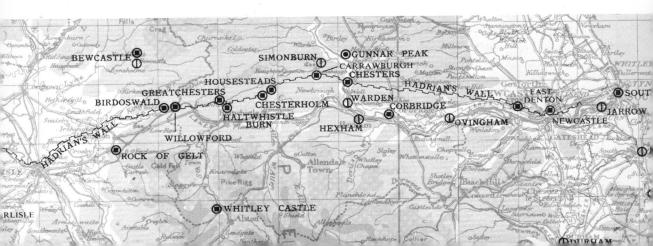

Chapter 11
Civilization and religion: the decline of Rome

We cannot leave the ancient world without saying something of
what was in many ways its greatest contribution to the ages which
were to follow. All the principal religions of today – apart from
Mohammedanism – developed within the ancient civilizations.

Hinduism

The main religion of India is Hinduism. Hindus worship many
different gods: gods of the sun, the moon, the sky and the storm;
the spirits of rivers, mountains, trees and animals. Some of these
gods seem to go back to the Indus Valley people; others were
brought by the Aryans when they invaded India about 1500 B.C.
All of them are still worshipped by various groups of Hindus
today.

With so many different gods, Hinduism may not seem to be
one religion at all. Yet it is. For, sometime between 1000 and
800 B.C., a great spiritual discovery was made, which ever since
has linked Hindus together.

At that time India had many holy men who turned away from
ordinary life and went to live deep in the heart of the forests,
where they could concentrate on spiritual things. Gradually these
holy men discovered yet another 'god'. But this one was entirely
different from the rest. They called him Brahman, which means
'the Supreme'; and they believed that he was the source and final
end of all life. This 'god' was not a person, but rather a universal
spirit. Brahman did not judge men, nor punish them. There was
no need to offer sacrifices to the Brahman; there was no need
to praise him or worship him either. He was beyond all other
gods; yet he was closer to man than any other god could possibly
be. What the holy men discovered was that this supreme spirit
was actually within themselves. By contemplation and spiritual
exercises they realized that their own souls were a part of
Brahman.

Naturally it was far from easy to reach this state of complete
holiness. The majority of Hindus had neither the time nor the
taste for long periods of silent meditation. So they continued to
worship the old gods as before by means of sacrifices, prayers
and festivals. Yet, with the discovery of Brahman, there was an

Siva, a Hindu god who may have been worshipped from the time of the Indus Valley civilization (see page 84). The god is shown in the dance of the universe, through which he crushes evil, represented by the dwarf under his feet, and creates good. His four arms show that he has many different powers.

important difference even for these people. For the holy men declared that all the traditional Hindu gods were really lower forms of this same universal spirit.

It was this idea which united the many branches of Hinduism into one great religion. The different groups of Hindus, serving their different gods, were like so many separate rivers; but in the end they all flowed into the one ocean which was Brahman.

Nevertheless it was believed that only certain Hindus could know the Brahman directly. Indian society was divided into four classes or castes. The professional priests, or Brahmins, formed the highest caste; next came the kings and nobles; then a caste consisting of merchants and professional men. Anybody belonging to

197

these upper castes could become a holy man and discover the Brahman. But those belonging to the lowest caste, that of peasants and servants, could not.

It is a very odd thing that whereas Christians long to be 'born again', and for a life after death, the aim of most Hindus is exactly the reverse. What the Hindu wants to do is to avoid being born again. For him salvation does not mean being admitted to heaven; it means escaping existence altogether. A holy man hopes that when he dies he will cease to be an individual person, but that his inmost soul will be completely lost and dissolved in the universal spirit – just as a grain of salt is lost and dissolved in water.

Hindus of the lowest caste, as well as members of the upper castes who failed to discover Brahman, were unable to escape existence in this way. Instead it was believed that they would be born again. If they had lived a good life they would be reborn into a higher caste; if a bad one, they would return to earth as an animal or an insect. This cycle of rebirths would go on until eventually they became holy men and discovered the true Brahman. Only then could they escape from the wheel of existence.

This Brahmin priest wears across his left shoulder the white sacred thread of the 'twice-born', indicating that he belongs to the upper castes. The bands of three white lines on his body and forehead show that he is a worshipper of Siva.

Giving the sacred thread of the 'twice-born' to the son of a Brahmin, when he reaches the age of nine or ten. This 'confirmation' ceremony introduces the boy to the priestly rites of the Brahmins. When he has received the sacred thread he will wear it over his shoulder at all times (see illustration above).

Buddha in a characteristic
pose. This bronze statue is
dated about 7th century A.D.

Buddhism

In the middle of the sixth century B.C. there lived in north-eastern
India a young man called Gotama. He was fortunate in many
ways, for his father was a prince who ruled a small district on
the slopes of the Himalayas. Before he was nineteen he had
married a beautiful cousin. Gotama lived in great comfort; he
loved his wife deeply, and had plenty of time for leisure. He ought
to have been one of the happiest people on earth. Yet he was not
happy; and this worried and puzzled him. He kept asking himself,
'Why am I not completely happy?'

While he was in this state he met a wandering holy man, who
had turned his back on the pleasures of the world in order to
search for a deeper spiritual happiness. Gotama felt a strong
desire to follow him.

At about the same time he met a man riddled with disease; an
aged man, crippled and shaking; and finally a corpse. These
pitiful sights reduced Gotama to extreme despair. They made
him realize how full the world was of suffering. They made him
realize also that his easy-going life could never satisfy him.

He thought again of the holy man. And suddenly Gotama's
mind was made up. A son had recently been born to him. No
matter. He would leave his family and his home. He would devote
his life to searching after some spiritual way of conquering pain
and suffering.

Gotama took a sad farewell of his wife and child while they
were still sleeping. Then he escaped into the woods, cut off his
hair, and changed his own rich clothes for those of a beggar.

After many years of meditation and experiment Gotama found
the secret wisdom for which his soul had always yearned. He
began to preach his message to those about him and soon had a
large number of disciples.

According to Gotama, the only way for a man to escape from
suffering was by killing his own selfishness; by giving up every
worldly desire and ambition. If people could once stop craving
after earthly things, they would eventually discover a true and
lasting serenity within themselves; and their souls would lapse
into a state of complete peace and oblivion.

This blissful condition which Gotama had discovered was
really the same as that which the Hindu holy men had long
known. But whereas they called it Brahman, he called it Nirvana.
And whereas the Hindus believed that only the three upper castes
could enjoy this supreme happiness, Gotama declared that everybody could reach it, whatever their race or their caste. Moreover

Left: Buddha before his enlightenment. According to Buddhist scriptures Gotama meditated for six years before he found enlightenment. During this time he ate so little that his body almost wasted away. In this carving disciples of the Buddha offer him food.

all who entered Nirvana would escape at death from the terrible wheel of rebirth. Because he had found the secret of sorrow and how to overcome it, Gotama was called the Buddha, which means 'the Fully Enlightened One'.

Buddhism spread throughout India and then overseas to Ceylon, Burma, Siam, China and Japan. In India itself the Hindu Brahmins were jealous of the new religion, since it challenged their own superiority. They did all they could to oppose it; and in the end Buddhism was driven out altogether. But in other eastern lands it has remained a great and powerful religion right down to the present day.

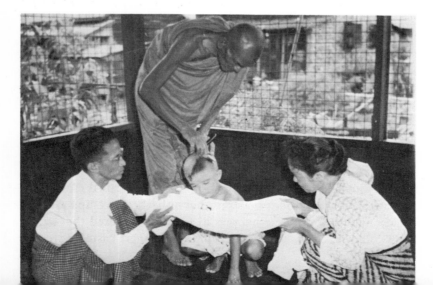

A Burmese Buddhist boy has his head shaved, symbolizing the Buddha's renunciation of worldly wealth.

Portrait of Confucius.

Confucianism

The Buddha lived in the sixth century B.C. In the same century Thales was laying the foundations of Greek learning; and among the Hebrews, Isaiah was foretelling the birth of the Messiah. Meanwhile, in far-away China, there was living yet another great teacher whose name was Confucius.

Confucius had a very different attitude to life from the Buddha. The Buddha was so horrified by all the suffering there was, that he taught men to cut themselves off from the world altogether.

Confucius was also concerned about the problem of suffering. But he thought that, instead of withdrawing into themselves, men ought to face their difficulties. It was true that pain and grief and misfortune could never be completely avoided. The good man, however, would be able to find the strength and courage to endure his tribulations.

In any case Confucius believed that much of the unhappiness in the world was unnecessary, for it was brought on by man's own folly and wickedness. So he concentrated on trying to teach better rules of conduct. He stressed the importance of family life, and insisted that people should be kind and considerate to their fellow men. Courtesy and gentlemanly behaviour, he believed, had a vital part to play in human affairs. In the China of his day only the wealthy were thought of as gentlemen. But Confucius taught that any man could be a gentleman, if his conduct were noble, unselfish and kind. Being a gentleman was not a matter of birth, but of character.

Confucius had little to say to the Chinese about God; nor was he much interested in what would happen to the soul after death. The thing that interested him was this world, not the next. 'While you cannot serve men,' he once argued, 'how can you serve spirits?'

The teachings of Confucius have continued to influence the personal behaviour of the Chinese, whether Confucians or not, right down to the present day; while all over the world Confucius is famous for his many wise sayings. Here are four of them:

'Virtue never dwells alone; it always has neighbours.'

'To see the right and not to do it is cowardice.'

'The wise man desires to be slow to speak but quick to act.'

'Do not do to others what you would not like yourself.'

Christianity

This last saying reminds us of Jesus, the founder of Christianity, who was born almost 600 years after the Buddha and Confucius.

Jesus was born in Palestine, a province of the Roman Empire, during the reign of its first emperor, Augustus Caesar. He was a person of intense spiritual power, who gave to mankind a message which was as far-reaching as it was simple. God was a loving father, he announced, and all men were brothers. Men must love and serve God; and this they could best do by loving and serving each other.

Jesus was a member of the Jewish race, his God was the Jewish God, and he based his new teachings on the old Jewish scriptures. But just as the Hindu priests rejected the Buddha, so – realizing that his ideas were a threat to their own power – the Jewish priests rejected Jesus. In the end the Roman governor, Pontius Pilate, allowed his crucifixion.

At that time Jesus had been preaching for only three years. Yet he had already gathered about him a small but determined band of disciples, and these men devoted their lives to the spreading of his message.

In this work they were joined by St Paul, a man whose ideas were to have almost as great an influence on the future of Christianity as the teachings of Jesus himself.

It was Paul who linked the story of Jesus to the story of the fall of man, which is found in the Book of Genesis. According to this, God originally created man perfect; and Adam and Eve had lived in a state of Paradise where sin, unhappiness and death were unknown. But then Adam disobeyed God by eating the forbidden fruit. He was turned out of Paradise, and all later men were born sinful.

By means of the fall story, Paul and other early Christians stressed man's sinfulness far more than Jesus had done. But they also stressed that, in sacrificing himself upon the cross, Christ had taken away the sin of Adam. Hence, for those who became Christians, Paradise was again open to man.

At first they supposed that this new Paradise, like the original one, would be on the earth itself, and that Jesus would come a second time to rule over it. But after a while, since this did not happen, they concluded that believers would only be restored to Paradise after death.

St Paul and the other early missionaries travelled to many parts of the Roman empire preaching their message of love and redemption. Everywhere they went they made converts, whom

Above: one of the earliest known representations of the Crucifixion of Jesus Christ. It comes from an ivory casket of about A.D. 400.
Below: a later painting of about A.D. 1250. The Crucifixion is one of the most important subjects of Christian art throughout history.

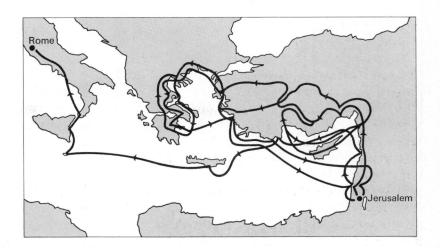

Right: St Paul's journeys. The apostle concentrated mainly on spreading the gospel to the lands of the eastern Mediterranean. Towards the end of his life, however, he made a journey to Rome. Compare this map with a modern atlas and make a list of the countries which St Paul visited.

they were careful to organize into local groups, or churches, each under its own leaders.

There were many different faiths in the Roman Empire at this time, and it was completely against the principles of the imperial government to punish people for their religious views. Roman citizens could worship any god they liked. On the other hand, whatever their private religion, all were expected to take part in the public festivals that were held for the worship of the emperor.

But this the Christians refused to do, since their scriptures strictly forbade them to acknowledge any but the one true God. It was chiefly for this reason that the Romans began to persecute them.

The first emperor to do so was Nero in A.D. 64. Tacitus, a Roman writer who lived at this time, tells us what happened:

First, Nero had self-acknowledged Christians arrested. Then, on their information, large numbers of others were condemned. . . . Dressed in wild animals' skins, they were torn to pieces by dogs, or crucified, or made into torches to be ignited after dark as substitutes for daylight. Nero provided his Gardens for the spectacle, and exhibited displays in the Circus, at which he mingled with the crowd – or stood in a chariot dressed as a charioteer. Despite their guilt as Christians, and the ruthless punishment it deserved, the victims were pitied. For it was felt that they were being sacrificed to one man's brutality rather than to the national interest.

Such persecutions broke out from time to time for another two and a half centuries. But the more Christians were persecuted

the more staunch they became in their faith; and, astonished by their determination and courage, the more eagerly others flocked to join them.

Eventually, there were so many Christians that they could be persecuted no longer. In A.D. 313 the first Christian emperor, Constantine, granted them complete freedom of worship and a few years later Christianity was made the official religion of the Roman empire.

From early times Christians in each district had elected their own leader or bishop. Naturally, the most important and influential district was Rome itself; and therefore the Bishop of Rome was able to claim that he was the leading priest of the Church. He became known as the Pope, a word meaning 'father'.

Christians in the eastern part of the empire, however, objected to this claim. Constantine had built a new Christian city at the Dardanelles, which was named Constantinople, after him. In the course of time, the bishop of this city became the head of an independent Eastern Church.

The fall of the Roman empire

While the Christian Church was marching from strength to

The catacombs were long burial galleries cut into the soft sandstone cliffs outside Rome. Apart from using them for burials the early Christians often worshipped in the catacombs and, in times of persecution, took refuge in secret passages.

strength, the Roman state was becoming weaker and weaker. The empire had enjoyed its greatest period of peace and prosperity during the second century A.D. In the third century, by contrast, there were frequent civil wars, as ambitious generals fought each other to decide who should be emperor. By this time, too, Roman citizens seemed to be losing interest in the empire to which they belonged. Consequently it became increasingly difficult to recruit men for the civil service and the legions.

It was hardly the time for such disunity and half-heartedness. All along the Rhine and Danube, various Germanic peoples, like the Franks, the Vandals and the Goths, were raiding across the frontiers of the empire.

These northern barbarians knew nothing of city life and, as far as civilization is concerned, were a good thousand years behind the Romans. Yet they were more than their equals in vitality, determination and fighting spirit. And they were desperate, too, since other savage hordes were pushing them from behind. The most terrifying of these were the Huns, a fearful Mongolian people whose original home had been on the borders of China. But at this time many of the peoples of northern Europe and northern Asia were on the march. The pressure was building up against the frontiers of the Roman Empire.

In such a desperate situation, commanding the whole empire seemed too much for one man. So it was decided that there should be two emperors, one ruling the west from Rome, the other ruling the east from Constantinople.

The eastern half managed to withstand the barbarian assaults. But in the west it proved quite impossible for the legions to keep out the invaders. At first some of the tribes were 'invited' to settle inside the empire, in the hope that they would help to drive the others off.

But this only advertised Rome's weakness; and like a great flood tide, the barbarian hordes came on. In 410 the Eternal City itself was sacked; and the whole west lay at their mercy. The Goths captured Italy and Spain. The Franks and Burgundians took possession of Gaul. The Vandals eventually fought their way into north Africa. Meanwhile, Britain had been abandoned by the legions, and was gradually conquered and settled by the Angles and Saxons.

St. Jerome wrote,

The mind shudders when dwelling on the ruin of our day. For twenty years and more, Roman blood has been flowing ceaselessly over the broad countries between Constantinople and the Julian Alps, where

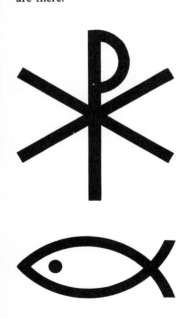

A Chrismon and a fish, two early symbols used by Christians. According to legend the Chrismon appeared in a dream to the Emperor Constantine. The sign is composed of the Greek initial letters of Christ, 'X' and 'P'. The fish derives from the fact that the Greek word 'fish' comes from the initial letters of Jesus Christ, Son of God, and Saviour (in Greek). What other symbols of Christ are there?

the Goths, the Huns and the Vandals spread ruin and death. . . . On every side is sorrow, on every side lamentation, everywhere the image of death.

As far as Europe was concerned, the Roman empire was at an end. But the Eastern Roman empire, based on Constantinople, survived for another thousand years. So throughout the centuries when the west was submerged in barbarian darkness, there remained in the east a secure refuge of civilization.

Nor in Europe itself were things quite so black as they seemed. The barbarians were uncouth, unlettered and uncivilized; yet they brought into the lands they conquered a new vitality and zest for life.

The barbarians destroyed the empire, but they did not destroy many of the things for which it had stood. We have seen before that when backward peoples conquer a more highly civilized race, it is generally the vanquished who turn out in the end to have done the real conquering. And so it was to prove again.

From the outset the barbarians were impressed by the achievements of Rome and proud to call themselves its heirs. Above all, they were impressed by the Roman Church. Before many centuries had passed, the whole of Europe had been converted to Christianity, and during the Dark Ages, the Church gradually taught the barbarians civilized ways. Meanwhile the monasteries kept alive the great tradition of classical learning.

Thus, in the course of time, a new civilization – the Western Christian civilization – was brought to birth. And once again the rich heritage of the ancient world was preserved and handed on.

Dates to remember

before 800 B.C.	Hindus discover Brahman
6th century B.C.	The Buddha and Confucius living
about A.D. 30	The crucifixion of Jesus
A.D. 410	The sack of Rome

Things to discuss

In what ways are the ancient civilizations we have discussed in this book important to us?

Things to do

1 Describe some of the ways in which Hinduism is different from Christianity.

2 The Romans have a great reputation for fairness and justice. Read the story of the trial of Jesus before Pontius Pilate and say whether you think it was conducted fairly.

3 Turn back to page 199 and study again the extract from Tacitus. In what ways were the Christians put to death? How did Nero react to the spectacle? Did all Romans react in the same way? Do you think Tacitus himself was a Christian?

4 From other books, find out as much as you can about the Roman emperor, Constantine. Write a brief biography of him.

Books to read

A. C. Bouquet, *Everyday Life in New Testament Times*, Batsford
Joseph Gaer, *How the Great Religions Began*, New English Library

The main religions of the world, except for tribal religions in Africa, Siberia and Indonesia, and the Jews, who are widely scattered. Two other important religions, although they are not widely practised, are Taoism in China and Shinto in Japan.

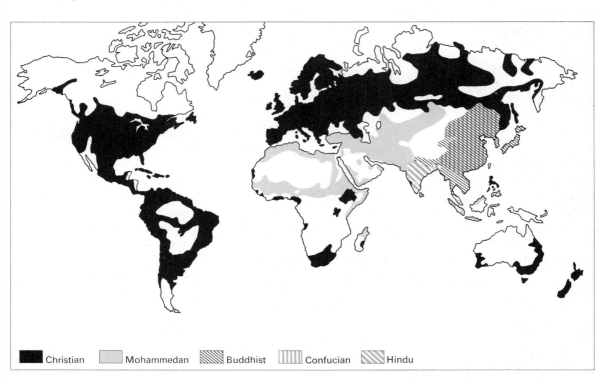

Christian Mohammedan Buddhist Confucian Hindu

Index

Numbers listed in italics (e.g. *15*) refer to the captions of illustrations.

Acknowledgements

ILLUSTRATION ACKNOWLEDGEMENTS

Aerofilms Limited: 186, 188, 189
Ashmolean Museum: Department of Antiquities: 31, 46, 146, 169, 172, 173, 177. Griffith Institute: 66, 67, 70
Associated Press Limited: 196
Bath Roman Museum: 187
Bibliothèque National, Paris: 152
British Museum: 21, 38, 43, 44, 45, 52, 58, 65, 69, 70, 71, 72, 73, 75, 77, 82/83, 85, 86, 88, 95, 99, 100, 106, 109, 116, 117, 121, 123, 125, 131, 133, 134, 137, 138, 139, 145, 147, 151, 154, 162, 163, 167, 170, 172, 175, 178, 179, 187, 195, 197, 198
British Museum (Natural History): 8, 10, 11, 12, 14, 15, 16/17, 27, 29, 170
Cheddar Caves: 16/17
Central Office of Information: 114, 175, 177
French Government Tourist Office: 19
Guildhall Museum: 180
D. A. Harissiadis: 89
John Hillelson Agency Limited: 9
India House: 79
Iraq Petroleum Company: 44, 51, 94, 105
Jena Museum: 50
Dr K. M. Kenyon: 30, 31
Mansell Collection: 19, 60, 84, 90, 92, 96, 102, 112, 113, 114, 118, 120, 129, 135, 137, 138, 139, 147, 156, 158, 159, 160, 161, 163, 165, 166, 167, 196, 200
Ministry of Public Building and Works: 171, 173, 174, 183, 185, 190/191
Metropolitan Museum of Art, New York: 193
Musées Nationaux: 16, 21
Museo Egizio, Turin: 76

National Museum of Wales: 176
National Tourist Organization of Greece: 118, 119 (photo N. K. Kontos), 149
Ordnance Survey: 191
Oriental Institute of the University of Chicago: 33, 49
Paul Popper Ltd: 63, 68, 80/81, 81, 82, 84, 141, 194
Réunion des Musées Nationaux: 144/145
Science Museum: 59
Staatliche Museen: 142
Thames and Hudson: 36
University Museum of Archaeology and Ethnology, Cambridge: 83
University Museum, Philadelphia: 40, 48/49
Victoria and Albert Museum: 106
Jacques Villeminot: 22
Wellcome Trust: 61, 143
Miss M. Wight: 170, 185
Roger Wood: 56, 57
Sir Leonard Woolley: 80

ARTISTS' CREDITS

David Nash: 42, 127
Gillian Newing: 41, 47, 50, 56, 74, 93, 107, 184, 201
Penguin Education Art Department: 13, 23, 24, 26, 28, 35, 37, 39, 55, 78, 87, 99, 101, 104, 111, 115, 122, 132, 153, 155, 157, 169, 171, 181, 189, 199, 203
Edward Poulton: 30, 46, 51, 63, 68, 108, 135, 140, 155, 182
Robert A. Sedgley: 16, 33, 40, 61, 64, 69, 91, 92, 136, 182
John Tyler: 62, 164